The Potential and Limitations of Bitcoin and Ethereum

S Thomas Zhang

The Potential and Limitations of Bitcoin and Ethereum

A Framework to Assess Blockchain Projects
from a Business and Economics Perspective

S Thomas Zhang

ISBN 978-3-031-56782-7   ISBN 978-3-031-56783-4   (Ebook)
https://doi.org/10.1007/978-3-031-56783-4

This Palgrave Macmillan imprint is published by the registered company Springer Nature Switzerland AG
The registered company address is: Gewerbestrasse 11, 6330 Cham, Switzerland

Paper in this product is recyclable.

PREFACE—THE NEEDS IN BLOCKCHAIN PRACTICE

Blockchain is a socio-technical invention. But there is currently no systematic discussion of the interdisciplinary concepts that fit together to explain how it works. This book formulates and discusses the interdisciplinary and intertwining concepts that make up blockchain and its functions in society, starting from the social and technical circumstances that inspired it, and without assuming any previous knowledge of the subject from the reader.

Then, this book distils the central non-technical concepts of blockchain into a framework summarized as the "EBC Pyramid".

This book has contributed to practice in two ways.

First, blockchain development has lacked conceptual guidance from non-technical fields. For example, a lot of recent efforts in blockchain have focused on solving technical challenges and building programming tools without regard to actual problems in society to address. While engineering advances can be inherently valuable, the most promising use of engineering effort is to address existing needs in society. There are economic, political, and legal problems that blockchains may address in society without fundamental advances in algorithm research. With the conceptual proposals in this book, engineering efforts might be directed more productively.

Second, and more practically, blockchains have become a new investment arena. The way most blockchain projects relies on incentives for participation means there is an investment market in cryptocurrencies from blockchain projects. These cryptocurrencies have made many people either wealthy or guilty. There is now an increasing need for systematic and reasoned blockchain analysis to assess and evaluate cryptocurrencies and blockchain projects. Indeed, an interdisciplinary conceptual understanding of blockchain will lead to more reasoned criteria in judging blockchain applications.

For the two purposes above, this book ultimately presents through its discussions a summarized "EBC Pyramid" framework. This framework distills the most relevant non-technical concepts that affect the viability and potential of blockchain applications. There is no other framework on this at the moment, and such a conceptual framework is much needed.

This EBC Pyramid framework, it is hoped, gives a structure to assist in the evaluation, critique, and otherwise discussion of individual blockchain applications. It is phrased as a few non-technical questions to consider when looking to start, participate in, or otherwise examine a particular blockchain application. The book then uses this framework to propose the possible non-technical foundations of Bitcoin and Ethereum. It is hoped the reader find the discussions and framework useful in an emerging world of blockchains.

CONTENTS

CHAPTER 1

Bitcoin History and Purpose

Abstract This chapter discusses the history and origins of blockchains from Bitcoin. It goes through the ideological conception of Bitcoin as an irreversible digital payment currency. It discusses the failures of previous attempts at digital currencies such as e-Gold and Bitcoin's likely inspiration from the BitTorrent technology used in the mid-2000s to circumvent copyright laws.

Keywords Bitcoin · Nakamoto · Cypherpunks · Decentralization

1.1 BITCOIN

Bitcoin is now quite well known as a digital payment system. The Bitcoin system is relatively easy to use. Anyone can download the Bitcoin software from www.bitcoin.org and create a Bitcoin address to send and receive Bitcoins with. Each new Bitcoin address (and one can create as many as one desires) comes with a corresponding password. Each address can receive Bitcoins freely but sending the Bitcoins held in an address requires having the password for that address. In this way, a Bitcoin address is very similar to a bank account holding a Bitcoin balance. Also similar to a bank account, one would need the account password to pay out of it.

S. T. Zhang, *The Potential and Limitations of Bitcoin and Ethereum*, https://doi.org/10.1007/978-3-031-56783-4_1

1

The key difference, though, is that there is no bank in the Bitcoin system. In fact, no single person or entity is formally in charge. Each Bitcoin address settles Bitcoin transfers with any other address directly based purely on the software. Fundamentally, this is all there is to Bitcoin. On the face of it, then, this may not seem to be much of a technological advance at all, let alone one that deserves any attention. Indeed, the only curiosity it seems to merit is why the artificial Bitcoin tokens can be worth any real money. After all, these Bitcoin balances are nothing more than transferable tokens in a virtual system, without any direct use even in its own virtual world. Yet, various websites and exchanges can allow the purchase or sale of Bitcoin from or into all major traditional (or "fiat") currencies such as US dollars, Euros, or pounds sterling. At the time of writing, each whole unit of Bitcoin is worth around $25,000,[1] making the collective Bitcoin balances of the entire system worth over $500 billion.

However, the nature of the Bitcoin technology is not always well-understood (Vergne & Swain, 2017). Technologically, as we shall soon understand more, Bitcoin was not much of an innovation. The innovation is more organizational and social. As various disciplines begin to form views towards Bitcoin and blockchain-related technologies (e.g. Mai et al., 2016; Wang & Vergne 2017), it is important to understand the nature of Bitcoin and other blockchain technologies and their potential so that they can be judged and discussed.

The conception of Bitcoin was rather new, in both concept and terminology (but perhaps not so much in technology), so a full appreciation of it is difficult to summarize as there has been nothing quite like it before. For the same reason, to fully understand it, a definition of the word "blockchain" takes some preliminary discussion. While accurate and insightful introductions to Bitcoin do exist (e.g. Böhme et al. 2015), they invariably leave out much technical detail or social context that will assist a fuller understanding and discussion. There has not been a short yet detailed enough discussion of how Bitcoin and related blockchain technologies work for a full picture of its nature.

This chapter covers some history and motivation of Bitcoin. Along the way, the terminology is explained as they are used in relation to Bitcoin and blockchains. The key innovation and defining feature of the Bitcoin system and for blockchain-driven systems, in general, is the feature of

---

[1] Dollars in this work refer to US dollars unless otherwise stated.

decentralization. That is, no single entity is formally responsible for the technology's operations and functioning. To understand the nature of Bitcoin and decentralized technologies, it is important to appreciate the initial motivation of Bitcoin as a payment system.

1.2   Nakamoto's Motivation for Bitcoin

Bitcoin began as a short "whitepaper" published online by Satoshi Nakamoto—well accepted to be a pseudonym—in 2008. Only 9 pages long, Nakamoto (2008) presented the idea of implementing a digital payment token that would go on to become Bitcoin. In this whitepaper, the author did not show any motivation for any type of anti-establishment goals, nor did he (pronoun used for convenience) indicate any grand vision of Bitcoin as an alternative monetary system.

Instead, the main problem Nakamoto wanted to solve was making small non-reversible digital payments:

> Commerce on the Internet has come to rely almost exclusively on financial institutions serving as trusted third parties to process electronic payments. While the system works well enough for most transactions, it still suffers from the inherent weaknesses of the trust based model. Completely non-reversible transactions are not really possible, since financial institutions cannot avoid mediating disputes. The cost of mediation increases transaction costs, limiting the minimum practical transaction size and cutting off the possibility for small casual transactions, and there is a broader cost in the loss of ability to make non-reversible payments for nonreversible services. With the possibility of reversal, the need for trust spreads. Merchants must be wary of their customers, hassling them for more information than they would otherwise need. A certain percentage of fraud is accepted as unavoidable. These costs and payment uncertainties can be avoided in person by using physical currency, but no mechanism exists to make payments over a communications channel without a trusted party. (p. 1, Nakamoto, 2008)

Based on the quote above, it is sometimes joked, but with a substantial element of believability, that Nakamoto was primarily interested in a way to pay for modestly priced pornography online without having to give out his credit card information. Indeed, as Nakamoto rightly points out, paying in physical cash for a pornography magazine in a shop does not require filling out a form and creating an account, but buying the same material digitally needs an online account and a credit card.

Why is there this difference? Nakamoto says it is because cash is final in physical transactions—if one takes a magazine and pays for it in cash, the deal is done and final. In contrast, according to Nakamoto, online buyers have the issue of a website taking payment but failing to deliver the pornography. Alternatively, if the pornography is delivered first, the buyer can then refuse to pay. So online, Nakamoto is saying, there is always a small amount of dispute about payments or refunds that then makes it necessary to get everyone's personal details for every transaction so that the parties can be found again in case of dispute.

Nakamoto notes that this is particularly problematic for small transactions (maybe for bits of pornography), where the transaction fee to pay for potential dispute resolution becomes big relative to the transaction itself.

Nakamoto was sufficiently bothered by this issue that he proposed the system of Bitcoin, which he believed would solve this issue.

Nakamoto was not entirely correct. As we shall see, Bitcoin did not solve the issue he raised.[2] But Nakamoto ended up, perhaps unexpectedly, creating a trillion-dollar market for cryptocurrencies, any of which can now conceivably be used to pay for online pornography without giving out personal credit card information.

1.3   BITCOIN FOR A BIGGER GOAL

Nakamoto's desire to buy pornography online without a credit card coincided with a bigger desire from more ideological technologists and the two camps combined in the corners of the web.

It happened that technology enthusiasts have long envisioned a digital payment and currency system outside government control and outside traditional banking institutions. One of the earliest such groups of proponents was known as the "cypherpunks" (sic), who believed strongly in the freedom and privacy aspects that a digital currency system could provide (Assange, 2012; Hughes, 1993). Such a system was also spawned by a mistrust of traditional central banking policy. This motivation was

---

[2] Ethereum, as discussed later, may have come much closer.

especially prominent after the quantitative easing—or money printing—following the Financial Crisis of 2007–2008. It was thought that a digital currency system like Bitcoin could be outside the control of central banks and hence could not be inflated at its policy discretion.

It is believed Nakamoto was genial to this idea because, by the time he coded up Bitcoin to launch on 3 January 2009, he inked into the permanent Bitcoin records the following headline: "The Times 03/Jan/2009 Chancellor on brink of second bailout for banks".[3] This was the front-page headline of The Times newspaper on 3 January 2009. Enthusiasts have read into this as Nakamoto passing commentary on bank bailouts, and the entire Bitcoin system has since been linked to a school of thought that proposes Bitcoin as an alternative digital monetary system.

A more mundane explanation for this newspaper quote is that it is the equivalent of holding up the day's newspaper as a validated date stamp, The Times being a newspaper of record. A further curiosity from this historical quote is that Satoshi Nakamoto likely operated from the UK, given that The Times is a British daily newspaper.

The creation of Bitcoin was exciting to many. Because until the creation of Bitcoin on 3 January 2009, every conceived alternative digital currency system had failed to succeed. They failed to succeed not because of lack of use or support, but rather because of regulators.

The key aspect to Bitcoin's ultimate and likely continuing viability is achieving decentralization. The entire Bitcoin currency system is run and maintained without any formal centralized entity (Narayanan et al., 2016). The Bitcoin system runs off the collective computing resources of anybody who wishes to participate in the Bitcoin software. The software is also completely open-source and anyone can contribute new updates to it.

So, crucially, decentralization means no single entity is legally responsible for Bitcoin.

Technologically, decentralization affords the substantial advantage of resilience. The system can survive the failure of any individual computer in the network or even the failure of a majority of the computers. As long as at least one computer continues to run the software, the Bitcoin system can in theory survive and be revived. Thus, the irreversible shutdown of such a system with a distributed user base is highly unlikely.

---

[3] This is a comment found in the first part of the Bitcoin Blockchain, which will be explained later. This comment could only have been left by the creator of Bitcoin.

However, decentralization—of having no key legal or physical entity that is responsible for the system—also happens to be very effective in avoiding legal problems. Centralized systems that operate with any centralized point of control have had a painful history of government shutdowns and legal punishment for any identifiable individuals involved (Ly, 2014; Mullan, 2014). Examples of government-circumventing technology that had identifiable individuals included e-gold (digital currency), Napster (sharing of copyrighted music), and Megaupload (sharing of copyrighted video). All these technological projects experienced dramatic shutdowns and asset seizures by governments and subsequent legal sagas for the individuals responsible (Meek, 2007; Pepitone, 2011; Williams, 2012). This bleak fate of technologists who sought to operate outside government control is likely why the creator of Bitcoin used only the pseudonym Satoshi Nakamoto.

Decentralized technology, in contrast—notably the copyright-circumventing file-sharing system BitTorrent—has proven highly elusive to a government crackdown. Starting in 2001, BitTorrent has never been successfully taken down, despite powerful attempts by governments around the globe. High-profile legal action, government shutdowns, and police raids on individual entities involved with BitTorrent have occurred in countries such as Finland (Cullen, 2004), Hong Kong (Bradsher, 2005), Singapore (Liew, 2007), Slovenia (Van der Sar, 2006), Sweden (Kiss, 2009), and the USA (Borland, 2004). In each case, though, the decentralized BitTorrent network kept going because it does not depend on any individual entity (or even a majority of entities) to operate.

BitTorrent remains in operation even today, sharing a vast library of music, books, movies, software, and other files in flagrant violation of copyright laws. In contrast to centralized file-sharing systems such as Napster and Megaupload, BitTorrent uses decentralization by breaking every shared file into many pieces and storing them on the decentralized hard disks of many users running the software. Most of the time, a complete version of a copyrighted file is not downloaded from any single person and the size of the network also makes any single individual difficult to target. But the collective effect is sharing copyrighted files. To achieve decentralization, BitTorrent uses error-checking algorithms to easily check that reconstituted large files are correct. Indeed, for a file broken into 1000 pieces and stored on 1000 different computers, the difference of a single bit in any single piece can be quickly detected using error-checking algorithms so that the integrity of the reconstructed file can be maintained.

The experience of BitTorrent suggests that decentralization in the digital domain is both possible and resilient against government intervention. Satoshi Nakamoto likely named Bitcoin in homage to BitTorrent, and uses the same principles of decentralization and error-checking to create a system that happens to be immune to government interference. Since no single entity or person is running the system, there is nobody to arrest or sue. This happy coincidence is also the result of nobody in the Bitcoin system needing to give personal details, least of all to any centralized entity that is in control.

Thus, Bitcoin is a decentralized and anonymous system, with features that make its users and supporters almost impossible to identify. The story goes that this then satisfied Satoshi Nakamoto's desire to anonymously buy modestly priced online pornography. But it turns out that such a decentralized and anonymous system had far broader appeal after it was shown to work.

1.4   THE STATE OF BITCOIN

Bitcoin actually works as a payment system as far as the basics go. The system allows people to open Bitcoin account addresses and transfer Bitcoins to each other. That is about all it does. But it is the basics of a payment system. Crucially, all this is being done in a system that no single person controls and everyone is in theory anonymous.

Various privacy activists, anarchists, possibly criminals, and other enthusiasts all steadily welcomed Bitcoin as a decentralized and anonymous payment system that works. Since 2009, Bitcoin has withstood the test of time in its basic functionality. It has also shown its technological and regulatory resilience. Bitcoin itself has never been hacked and no government has been successful in shutting it down.

Many observers hailed it as a fundamental game-changer in the world order. May still believe that to be true. However, Bitcoin is still rather primitive. There are many things the Bitcoin system does not do. For example, there is no way to add any type of reference number or note to a Bitcoin transaction. So, an online shop that wanted to know which of two customers is paying would need to generate two separate Bitcoin addresses, one to give to each customer to pay. Bitcoin addresses are unlimited, so a lot of these features are bells and whistles that can be worked around as long as the basic functions work, and they do.

However, there are also many things that Bitcoin turns out not to be so good at after all. For example, Bitcoin is not very fast. Indeed, a Bitcoin payment is slower than a credit card payment. It takes at least 10 minutes or so to get a Bitcoin payment through, and often much longer, especially if one wishes to make sure it went through. Transaction fees for Bitcoin transactions are rather high so small transactions are not practicable, contrary to the initial motivation to create Bitcoin. Bitcoin only processes a somewhat fixed number of about 1000–4000 transactions every 10 minutes or so. Thus, at that pace, it is far from being able to handle the scale of daily transactional use globally.

Waiting a few hours for a Bitcoin payment to go through while paying a sizable transaction fee to buy some online pornography turns out not to be a good use of Bitcoin, contrary to the initial possible intent of the Bitcoin whitepaper. For similar reasons and more, Bitcoin makes for bad currency for most daily purposes.

Further discussion of Bitcoin and blockchain in general needs a more detailed understanding of the mechanisms of the Bitcoin system.

References

Assange, J. (2012). *Cypherpunks: Freedom and the future of the internet*. OR Books.

Böhme, R., Christin, N., Edelman, B., & Moore, T. (2015). Bitcoin: Economics, technology, and governance. *Journal of Economic Perspectives, 29*(2), 213–238.

Borland, J. (2004, December 20). BitTorrent file-swapping networks face crisis. *CNET*.

Bradsher, K. (2005, November 8). In Hong Kong, a jail sentence for online file-sharing. *The New York Times*.

Cullen, D. (2004, December 14). Finnish police raid BitTorrent site. *The Register*.

Hughes, E. (1993). *A cypherpunk's manifesto*. Retrieved January 31, 2018, from https://www.activism.net/cypherpunk/manifesto.html

Kiss, J. (2009, April 17). The Pirate Bay trial: Guilty verdict. *The Guardian*.

Liew, H. (2007, September 30). Parents get shock letter. *The New Paper*.

Ly, K. M. (2014). Coining Bitcoin's 'legal-bits': Examining the regulatory framework for Bitcoin and virtual currencies. *Harvard Journal of Law and Technology, 27*(2), 587–608.

Mai, F., Bai, Q., Shan, Z., Wang, X., & Chiang, R. (2016). *From Bitcoin to Big Coin: The impacts of social media on Bitcoin performance* (Working Paper).

Meek, J. G. (2007, June 3). Feds out to bust up 24-karat web worry. *New York Daily News.*

Mullan, P. (2014). *The digital currency challenge: Shaping online payment systems through US financial regulations.* Palgrave Macmillan.

Nakamoto, S. (2008). *Bitcoin: A peer-to-peer electronic cash system.* Retrieved January 31, 2018, from www.bitcoin.org

Narayanan, A., Bonneau, J., Felten, E., Miller, A., & Goldfeder, S. (2016). *Bitcoin and cryptocurrency technologies: A comprehensive introduction.* Princeton University Press.

Pepitone, J. (2011, November 30). Today is Napster's last day of existence. *CNN.*

Van der Sar, E. (2006, December 19). Suprnova.org: Two years since the shutdown. *TorrentFreak.*

Vergne, J.-P., & Swain, G. (2017). Categorical anarchy in the U.K.? The British media's classification of Bitcoin and the limits of categorization. *Research in the Sociology of Organizations, 51,* 185–222.

Wang, S., & Vergne, J.-P. (2017, January). Buzz factor or innovation potential: What explains cryptocurrencies' returns?. *PLoS One,* 12(1), e0177659.

Williams, C. (2012, January 20). Anonymous attacks FBI website over Megaupload raids. *The Telegraph.*

CHAPTER 2

Bitcoin Mechanisms and the Blockchain

Abstract This chapter provides a more in-depth discussion of the mechanism used to run the Bitcoin system and what it accomplishes. With accessible technical details, hash functions and cryptography are introduced. Then their application in Bitcoin is discussed to solve the particular problem of counterfeiting (or double-spending) in payment systems. This then leads to the role of Bitcoin's "proof-of-work" algorithm to make the system costly in real terms, and why that is important in terms of incentives.

Keywords Blockchain · BitTorrent · Trustless · Mining · Consensus · Hashcash · Proof-of-Work

2.1 THE BLOCKCHAIN

While Bitcoin might be named after the file-sharing system BitTorrent, Bitcoin aims to achieve almost the opposite technological goal of BitTorrent. Unlike BitTorrent, where the goal is to freely copy identical files among users, a digital currency system such as Bitcoin must essentially do the opposite and prevent users from counterfeiting—that is, copying—units of the currency. This is also known as the "double-spending" problem.

© The Author(s), under exclusive license to Springer Nature   11
Switzerland AG 2024
S. T. Zhang, *The Potential and Limitations of Bitcoin and Ethereum*,
https://doi.org/10.1007/978-3-031-56783-4_2

Historically, preventing currency counterfeiting required either irreplaceable physical currency (such as gold coins) or a trusted centralized entity (like a mint) with the sole enforceable authority to create the currency. In either case, each unit of the currency cannot be copied by the common user. But neither method is compatible with the goals of Bitcoin. First, Bitcoin is to be digital, and anything digital can be easily copied, so using something physical is out of the question. Second, Bitcoin was specifically intended to operate without a trusted central authority, so having an authorized type of mint is also not aligned with the goal. In relation to a mint, Bitcoin is even called "trustless" precisely because of not relying on any trusted centralized authority to validate the currency or any transactions between users. So how, then, can anyone tell the difference between an authentic Bitcoin and a copy of one? How can each legitimate unit of Bitcoin be made distinct from another?

Using a slight twist on an established concept,[1] Bitcoin solves this counterfeiting problem by keeping an *entirely public history of all recognized Bitcoin transactions from the very beginning of the Bitcoin system.* Thus, every Bitcoin would have a fully public chain of provenance. Any Bitcoin without such a chain of provenance is not valid and is rejected by the Bitcoin software. In fact, Bitcoin can be defined as a unique history of transactions on this public ledger of transactions (Nakamoto, 2008).

The complete history of Bitcoin transactions is kept in a large and fully *unencrypted* text file that is downloaded with the Bitcoin software to every computer in the Bitcoin network, and this file is subsequently updated approximately every 10 minutes on all computers with the addition of new "blocks" of transactions that have occurred since the previous update. Any transfer of Bitcoin is only recognized by computers in the system if the provenance of the Bitcoin can be traced in this history file to the Bitcoin address sending it. Nobody, then, can claim to have Bitcoin that does not have a publicly verifiable origin according to this public ledger file. The issue of "fake" Bitcoins is hereby solved.

This large transaction history file is called, famously, the "Blockchain". (In this book, the capitalized word "Blockchain" refers specifically to the Bitcoin system, and the word "blockchain" without capitalization refers to analogous files in other systems). The Blockchain literally contains the list

---

[1] The relevant concept is a chain of provenance. This is used sometimes in the art world. It is also used in land ownership when there is no centralised land registry.

of every transaction of all the Bitcoins in existence, from the very beginning—or "genesis"—of the Bitcoin system on 3 January 2009. Unlike files on BitTorrent, the Blockchain file is not broken into pieces. The Blockchain is stored as identical copies on every computer in the Bitcoin system, and regularly updated on each.

As computers transact Bitcoin, the Blockchain correspondingly gets bigger. A feature of the Blockchain is that it is updated approximately every 10 minutes with new chunks of transactions. Thus, the Blockchain is updated in 10-minute batches of transactions. Each of these batches is called a "block", the full sequence of which forms the Blockchain.

As a technical parameter without a specific reason, each block of new transactions is limited to 1 Mb in size. Further transactions beyond what can be recorded in 1 Mb will need to wait for a later block to be recorded onto the Blockchain (or not go through as a transaction at all). Hence, the Blockchain increases by about 1 Mb every 10 minutes. There is no limit on the total size of the Blockchain as it continues to grow forever in size. This is not regarded as a problem because the availability of storage is believed to continue to grow along with the growth of the Blockchain. Also, the speed of growth of the Blockchain is arithmetic rather than geometric, so is believed to be tractable. The current Blockchain is already large. At the time of writing, the Blockchain is over 500 Gb.

Thus, the entire Bitcoin system centers on this large text file called the Blockchain that updates every 10 minutes. By the definition of Bitcoin, this text file itself also keeps track of the balance of Bitcoins at each Bitcoin address. It is a point to note that the Bitcoin system is limited in the total number of transactions it can conduct by the 1 Mb block size limit.

Since the Blockchain contains the full transaction history of all Bitcoins, each Bitcoin today must have an origin somewhere on the Blockchain. That is, each Bitcoin must have spawned in one specific block and at one specific Bitcoin address. How is that determined?

Bitcoins are spawned in a Bitcoin address via a specific type of tournament game. Playing in the tournament is called "mining", and this creates new Bitcoins.

2.2   "Mining" for Bitcoin

New Bitcoins are allocated to accounts through a type of tournament game called Hashcash.[2] Computers in the Bitcoin network can choose to participate or not. Parameters of the game are set so that a winner is found about 10 minutes before the game starts again. The winner of each tournament gets a Bitcoin reward spawned into its associated Bitcoin address. This Bitcoin reward is currently 6.25 Bitcoins. So, every 10 minutes or so, a computer that is playing this tournament wins 6.25 Bitcoins. At current prices, this reward equates to about $170,000. Computers in the Bitcoin network that are playing this tournament are said to be "mining" for Bitcoin.

These mining tournament rewards are the only source of new Bitcoins. This reward began with 50 Bitcoins every 10 minutes in 2009 when the Bitcoin system started. The reward then halves approximately every 4 years. At this rate, the reward will reach a technical bound of 0 around the year 2140, when a total of 21 million Bitcoins will have been allocated via this tournament to computers in the system. Absent a software change on this, there will be no new Bitcoins after the year 2140. Many believe that this hard limit of 21 million Bitcoin is quintessential to the Bitcoin system and shall never be changed. At least for the foreseeable future, this tournament system is still creating new Bitcoins.

Since there is a substantial reward of Bitcoins for winning this tournament, there is a clear incentive for computers to join the Bitcoin network and play this game. This tournament is critical to the Bitcoin system. Bitcoin uses this tournament to spawn new Bitcoins. But more importantly, the system also uses this tournament as the rule to choose the next block to be on the Blockchain. The rules governing how the next block is to be added to the Blockchain are termed the "consensus protocol".

2.3   The Consensus Protocol

Regularly adding updates to a large file such as the Blockchain is not technically difficult in itself. What makes this task difficult is that Bitcoin is *decentralized*. So, if there is no central administrator, who decides which transactions go into the next block of the Blockchain?

---

[2] The actual Bitcoin system uses a variation of Hashcash.

The rule used to decide who adds the next block to the Blockchain is called Bitcoin's "consensus protocol". The Bitcoin protocol is simply that the winner of each Hashcash tournament also chooses which transactions to add to the next block of the Blockchain (in addition to getting the tournament reward). Since the Hashcash tournament is set to find a winner every 10 minutes or so, the Blockchain also adds a new block at the same rate.

Thus, roughly every 10 minutes, the Blockchain is expected to grow by another 1 Mb block of official transactions. At any time in between, computers—mining or not—that wish to transfer Bitcoin will broadcast their proposed transaction to the network.[3] Any mining computer in the network will then consolidate these proposed transfers into a pool that it catches and "proposes" a new block of transactions onto the Blockchain. These block proposals often differ. For example, when there are more proposed transactions than the size limit of the next block, different miners can propose blocks containing different transactions. But only one new block will be chosen from among them to be next on the Blockchain. So, the Bitcoin consensus protocol is to take the block proposed by the winner of the current Hashcash tournament.

If there are fewer than 1 Mb of new transactions—below the block size limit—then all transaction proposals could in principle be included in the next block, but there can still be differences in the order of transactions or if some proposed transactions did not reach some of the miners or if there were leftover transactions from the previous round. Furthermore, two mining computers can propose the same block of transactions, but only one of them will win the tournament and get the honor of putting the next block onto the Blockchain (along with the mining reward).

Can a miner ever win a round of the Hashcash tournament but not propose a new block? No, this is not possible. Because the entry ticket to the Hashcash tournament itself contains the proposed new block. So, the tournament winner is chosen among those who propose new blocks. The next section describes the mechanism of this Hashcash tournament in somewhat more detail.

---

[3] This broadcast is a routine procedure over computer networks. It is nothing particular to Bitcoin.

2.4   THE HASHCASH TOURNAMENT

The Hashcash tournament in Blockchain uses a "cryptographic hashing function" known as SHA-256. This function takes any amount of text and numbers and transforms it into a code that is exactly 256 characters long. This output code is called the "digest" of the input. Sometimes, the digest is called the "signature" of the input.

As an example, the digest of the entire previous paragraph is: 030fa9b349c51da9c9195eb1fb70fbf303177fc5315031ad04ca 3b3a8193ff7a
The digest of the digest above is:
8997debf01c4aab9dc89b9bc4573323fa6b8f81f3cab8b84f6b21dde 71f399a0
The digest of the number "2" by itself is:
d4735e3a265e16eee03f59718b9b5d03019c07d8b6c51f90da3a666eec 13ab35
The digest of the number "20" is:
f5ca38f748a1d6eaf726b8a42fb575c3c71f1864a8143301782de 13da2d9202b

A SHA-256 processor can easily be found with an internet search. As can be seen, there is no obvious relationship between the input and its digest. And there is no way to recover the original input from having only its 256-character digest. However, the same input always creates the same digest through SHA-256. Furthermore, small differences in the input will create very different digests, as can be seen in the digests above of 2 versus 20. Before Bitcoin, the SHA-256 function could be used, for example, to compare whether two files are exactly the same. Small differences can result in dramatically different digests.

In the Bitcoin system, a miner wins the Hashcash tournament by being the first to send out a proposed block with a corresponding 32-bit number called its **nonce** that, when put through SHA-256, results in a digest that satisfies the current tournament **difficulty threshold**. Note that a different proposed block will have a completely different nonce.

More specifically, the winner is the first computer to propose a new block together with a nonce such that the digest of the following combined block of text satisfies the current tournament difficulty threshold:

[Digest of the previous block] [contents of proposed block] [proposed nonce]

The difficulty threshold can be, for example, for a digest to start with 0 to win (and then be followed by 255 further characters). If this is the current difficulty threshold, the goal to win is to propose a block and a nonce so that they, together with the previous block's digest, produce an SHA-256 digest that starts with a 0 (followed by 255 other characters). Finding a nonce that, combined with the proposed block and the previous block digest, results in a digest that starts with 0 can only be found by trial and error. The computer would systematically take a block of proposed transactions try all possibilities of the nonce and feed them through the SHA-256 function to see if the digest starts with a 0. If no nonce works for a proposed block (which happens frequently), the computer will then try to change the proposed block slightly (such as changing the order of transactions) and then try that amended proposed block with all different combinations of the nonce. Once in a rare while, the computer will indeed find a combination of block and nonce that satisfies the difficulty threshold criterion. The computer will promptly broadcast the block-nonce pair to the network to see if it was the first to find a winner. If it is, it wins the tournament reward and its corresponding block (along with the nonce) will be added to the Blockchain. The Bitcoin software on all computers in the system is programmed to recognize a winner when it sees one.

The Bitcoin system calibrates the tournament difficulty threshold—for example by requiring the winning digest to start with 00 instead of 0— about every 2 weeks so that, on average, one computer satisfies it every 10 minutes. Thus, if many miners join the network and it takes a shorter time to find a winner, the system will scale the difficulty threshold parameters so that winning gets harder and takes longer, reverting to roughly 10-minute intervals. Similarly, if miners leave the network and it is taking longer to find winners, the system will set the difficulty threshold lower to make it easier and faster to win.

Finding a block and matching nonce by trial and error takes a lot of computation. In practice at the time of writing, the number of tries needed to win the race to get a block onto the Blockchain every 10 minutes can be orders of quintillions, which is a meaningful challenge for even the fastest computers. Being the first to deliver a winning block-nonce pair means the miner is very lucky or, far more likely, has spent a lot of effort by trial and error to find this pair.

Winning this tournament represents a lot of computational work. A computer that is playing this tournament noticeably burns a lot of electricity. Thus, being able to produce a winning block-nonce pair is "proof" that significant computational work was done. Because of this, choosing the winner of such a tournament to add the next block is called a "proof-of-work" consensus protocol. Bitcoin uses this Hashcash proof-of-work consensus protocol.

2.5   The Effect of Proof-of-Work

Computers mining Bitcoin participate in the Hashcash tournament. Every 10 minutes, only one such computer in the world will win the Bitcoin reward. This is very few. For an idea of scale, a high-end laptop doing full-time mining can expect a reward once in many years at the time of writing. Nonetheless, that win is about $170,000, so is still a decent prize. But practically, many computers may band together into pools to share computing power as well as any mining rewards.

Playing this tournament has become a huge global undertaking, especially in countries with relatively cheap electricity prices to run mining computers. The Cambridge Bitcoin Electricity Consumption Index[4] shows that Bitcoin mining globally is consuming more electricity than entire countries such as Chile, Sweden, or even possibly Spain.

Hashcash computations are fundamentally useless except to the extent that they identify winners to propose the next block on the Blockchain. The cost of the electricity running this system, and the corresponding greenhouse gases emitted to generate that electricity, has been subject to much debate and controversy. Is all this worth it? Is there not a better way?

There are, though, at least two reasons why Bitcoin and several other blockchain projects use proof-of-work consensus protocols to make it computationally costly to mine.

First, on average, the Bitcoin consensus protocol creates a Blockchain via the costliest path. Each block is added by a computer that, on

---

[4] https://ccaf.io/cbnsi/cbeci.

average, burned the most electricity in those 10 minutes of the corresponding tournament. This chain of highest cost makes it uneconomical for computers to try to re-mine the Blockchain to alter an earlier block. Doing so would incur at least as much electricity than what was originally used to mine it, so taking the costliest block in the initial mine will likely make it unprofitable for a later miner to try to alter the official Blockchain. Such a miner would likely prefer to use its computation power to mine the next block instead of re-mining a previous block.

Second, using computation is the way that Bitcoin can link its online digital balances to the tangible cost of a physical resource—namely, electricity. By using proof-of-work, Bitcoin has real physical resource costs to create. Thus, those who choose to mine it must be willing to spend the corresponding cost on physical resources. Bitcoin thus directly links itself to physical resource consumption rather than having a purely digital value. Some might argue that because it takes a certain amount of real electricity to produce each Bitcoin, Bitcoin should be worth at least a certain amount. Others would counter that just because valuable electricity was used in creating something like Bitcoin does not make the output necessarily valuable. After all, Bitcoin computations are not in themselves valuable, and generating large amounts of random numbers can burn electricity without creating value. It is easy to find examples of wasting electricity, like leaving the lights on all day, without anything useful to show for it.

2.6   Transaction Processing Fees

In addition to the Hashcash tournament reward described previously, there is one more incentive for miners to play in the tournament.

This is the transaction processing fee. Those who wish to send transactions can offer a transaction processing fee in Bitcoin to give to any miner who successfully puts that transaction onto the Blockchain. This transaction processing fee is added to the mining rewards of new Bitcoin given to the winner in each round, as it currently runs. As mentioned previously, when a total of 21 million Bitcoins have been created (at time of writing, over 19 million Bitcoins have already been created), there will be no more mining rewards in the form of new Bitcoins. Thus, after all the Bitcoin have been mined, all the mining incentives would come from transaction processing fees.

The role of this transaction processing fee is curious. Because it appears to function against Satoshi Nakamoto's original idea of a micro-payment system with very low transaction fees.

Because each block size on the Blockchain is 1 Mb, each block is limited to about 3000 transactions. Thus, there is a technical limit on the total number of transactions that the Blockchain supports. The number of Bitcoin addresses may be unlimited, but the entire system can only add 1 Mb of transactions every 10 minutes.

If Bitcoin grows in users, transactions per user on the Bitcoin network must necessarily decrease. This also means that transactions on the Blockchain will become more valuable, and thus transaction processing fees are likely to increase in size. In practice, at the time of writing, a transaction fee is already almost mandatory for a transaction to be mined. Transactions without fees offered are less likely to be prioritized by miners to the extent that they never get mined onto the Blockchain. This also means that more and more Bitcoin transactions between counterparties are being "netted" off the Blockchain with only the final netted amount sent for processing on the Blockchain. Transacting on the Blockchain is expensive and will likely get more so.

2.7   GLOBAL GOVERNANCE AND SYSTEM UPGRADES

On top of the consensus and incentive structures of Bitcoin lies high-level governance issues of how the entire Bitcoin system works. Everything about Bitcoin is encoded in software, and software can be changed. Bitcoin is a live open-source project on the GitHub website with code that anyone can contribute to. If that is the case, how can Bitcoin prevent malicious actors from changing the software? At the same time, how can legitimate software upgrades be implemented? Who decides which version of the software is the official version?

Changes to the Bitcoin software can alter the consensus protocol, the incentive structure, or any other aspect of the Bitcoin system. Many major changes became increasingly necessary. For example, a possible upgrade is to compress or otherwise reduce the size of the Blockchain, perhaps by splitting it into smaller chunks. Another example is to increase the existing block size or capacity. At the same time, there can be malicious changes such as a change to transfer all Bitcoin to one particular address.

As a decentralized system, Bitcoin ultimately relies on some type of majority voting to organize changes to the software itself. Whenever the

Bitcoin software is amended, users on the network must choose to download the new software or continue on the older version. The Bitcoin network will deem legitimate the version of the software—and hence the version of the Blockchain—that at least 50% of the computers (by mining power) are using. So, the Bitcoin system treats the majority choice as official. If somehow over 50% of the network runs a malicious or fraudulent version of the software (for example, a version that transfers all Bitcoins owned by the minority to the majority), then even this unscrupulous version will go through as official.

However, in this case of tyranny of the majority, the decentralization of Bitcoin offers a unique additional safeguard of sorts. The minority that was harmed can refuse to use the new software and continue to use the original software and the original Blockchain. Two Bitcoin systems will then be created with the two groups going separate ways with different blockchains into the future starting from the point of disagreement. The Blockchain, by its nature, has an infinite backup system so users can decide to continue in a different direction from any earlier point. When this happens—when the users decide to go separate ways with different software versions and different blockchains—it is called a "fork".

In fact, for decentralized technologies, instances of technological decisions resulting in disagreements that are not resolved are quite common. In such cases, entire systems may break off as forks into two or more branches, each with its own communities of supporters. By convention, the larger branch tends to keep the original name. Examples include the fork of Bitcoin Cash from Bitcoin and, subsequently, the fork of Bitcoin Gold from Bitcoin. A system called Bitcoin SV later forked out of Bitcoin Cash. Each of these forks was the result of disagreements on software features. All these systems run in parallel but the smaller forks tend to wither away over time.

Thus, in the decentralized Bitcoin system, because no single entity can unilaterally impose any changes, there is an important and distinctive element of democratic voting on possible new versions of the software. Software versions that only a minority of the computers in the network support will not be implemented. Such collective decision-making due to majority voting has been recognized in other contexts as inefficient (e.g. Arrow, 1950; Gibbard, 1973; Satterthwaite, 1975) and is a major deterrent to Bitcoin development in contrast to systems controlled by a centralized decision-maker. But the Bitcoin system also offers the unique remedy that the minority is free to fork out into their own system.

REFERENCES

Arrow, K. (1950). A difficulty in the concept of social welfare. *Journal of Political Economy, 58*(4), 328–346.

Gibbard, A. (1973). Manipulation of voting schemes: A general result. *Econometrica, 41*(4), 587–601.

Nakamoto, S. (2008). *Bitcoin: A peer-to-peer electronic cash system.* Retrieved January 31, 2018, from www.bitcoin.org

Satterthwaite, M. A. (1975). Strategy-proofness and Arrow's conditions: Existence and correspondence theorems for voting procedures and social welfare functions. *Journal of Economic Theory, 10*(2), 187–217.

CHAPTER 3

Other Blockchain Applications

Abstract This chapter provides an overview discussion of some other applications that are often associated with the use of blockchains. Blockchain projects and applications continue to proliferate at a fast pace. This is only a small sample of them. Many of the currently leading cryptocurrencies are mentioned along with a few defunct or minor ones.

Keywords Cryptocurrency · Stablecoin · CBDC · Scalability · Trilemma

3.1 BLOCKCHAIN APPLICATIONS AND CRYPTOCURRENCIES

The defining feature of Bitcoin is a decentralized network coordinated by a large shared document that all participants refer to, agree on, and collectively update based on an agreed rule. The agreement and updating rules are enforced through the software via cryptography. Such a document is known as a blockchain.

In essence, a blockchain is a large public spreadsheet file that users add new rows to over time. Which user gets to add new rows depends on the consensus rules, such as winning puzzle tournaments, which are designed to align incentives or achieve some overall goal for the system.

© The Author(s), under exclusive license to Springer Nature Switzerland AG 2024
S. T. Zhang, *The Potential and Limitations of Bitcoin and Ethereum*,
https://doi.org/10.1007/978-3-031-56783-4_3

23

The blockchain for Bitcoin simply keeps track of transactions between addresses. But with some thinking, such a shared document can be used to coordinate other decentralized activities.

In most of these blockchain projects, participants need to be incentivized to contribute some resource to maintaining the blockchain. Usually, as with Bitcoin, this is done via a system of internal fees or rewards. These blockchain projects thus commonly invent various exchangeable tokens—also called "coins", "altcoins", "cryptocurrencies", or "cryptoassets"[1]—to serve as units of these incentives. As with units of Bitcoin, units of these token rewards are completely arbitrary but their names often serve to identify the blockchain projects.

Because most blockchain projects have an associated token or cryptocurrency, they are often seen as necessary for all blockchains. However that is not the case, and the next chapter will present an example of a feasible blockchain application without any associated cryptocurrency.

Some categories of existing applications of blockchains are discussed next.

3.2   PAYMENT SYSTEMS

The most established use of blockchains are for payment systems, which was the original intent of Bitcoin.

Bitcoin itself has no direct use. The Bitcoin system does little aside from transferring Bitcoin between its own addresses. But if participants in the Bitcoin system—by some convention or market force—can agree that Bitcoins can be exchanged for some value in fiat currency or real goods, then Bitcoin can indeed serve as a valid payment system to keep track of transfers between owners of Bitcoin addresses. Furthermore, as intended with decentralization, this system is resilient against the failure of any specific part of the overall system. There is a lot of redundancy built in. Bitcoin as a payment system is fully in operation now, with Bitcoin having a clear (but volatile) market value against major fiat currencies such as the US Dollar.

Bitcoin has mostly withstood the test of time in the sense that it works from a technical perspective. The question of its economic use and value is discussed in a later chapter. The established and functional use of Bitcoin

---

[1] There may be some pedantic differences between these words, but they are mostly interchangeable.

as a payment system spawned several other payment systems based on the blockchain concept. These other payment systems are also the most functional of the blockchain projects that exist currently. Blockchain-driven payment systems do work in a technical sense, and almost every other blockchain project also has a built-in payment mechanism to transfer its tokens among users. Thus, most blockchain projects also have an embedded payment function.

Most of the other blockchain payment-only projects are designed in response to some perceived shortcomings in the Bitcoin design.

For example, one notable shortcoming of Bitcoin is that transfers are relatively slow and unsuitable for small sums (due to fees). It takes at least 10 minutes and often hours for a transaction to be added to the Blockchain and for this to be checked and confirmed, especially when the network is congested. Other blockchain projects such as Litecoin, Stellar, and Ripple are designed to process transactions faster and at lower fees. For example, Litecoin adds a new block of transactions every 2.5 minutes instead of Bitcoin's every 10 minutes.

A second notable shortcoming is that Bitcoin is deliberately wasteful in its computational requirements. There have been some earlier attempts (such as Curecoin or Gridcoin) that aimed to harness this computation for scientific research. But a more recent development is to change the Proof-of-Work consensus protocol. For example, Peercoin is a blockchain project that incorporates another consensus protocol termed Proof-of-Stake, where those who already hold more Peercoin have a higher chance at getting their proposed blocks added onto the blockchain (and hence earn a fee or reward). In a Proof-of-Stake system, the equivalent of "mining" is called "staking". Such a consensus protocol has been the subject of much debate on whether it naturally leads to centralization over time. Proof-of-Stake is supposed to eliminate the need for wasteful energy consumption and gives the most say to those who hold the most stake in protecting the system. However, there is a lending market for tokens in Proof-of-Stake systems, so borrowers can aggregate a borrowed balance to use to stake for rewards. The dynamics of how that plays out in the long term is not yet clear.

Other consensus protocols have also been proposed, such as Proof-of-Capacity, Proof-of-Association, Proof-of-Activity, and Proof-of-Burn. None is widely popular but all provide a rule on picking which user gets to add the next block update.

Finally, a third potential shortcoming of sorts is that the Bitcoin Blockchain is unencrypted and public. While individual addresses might be anonymous on the Blockchain, all transactions are fully traceable to every address. Certain blockchain projects such as Monero and Dash are payment coins that make transaction records verifiable but private on their blockchains. While it may sound contradictory to have a public ledger of transactions that is also private, cryptographic coding methods can leave a verifiable and auditable public record of a transaction without actually revealing the destination or origin of the transaction.

At the time of writing, many of the largest blockchain networks are designed purely for payment transfers. These include Bitcoin and its forks, Litecoin, Stellar, Ripple, and Monero. However, almost every cryptocurrency can serve a similar payment transfer purpose. Thus, pure-play payment transfer projects other than Bitcoin and stablecoins (discussed next) have steadily retreated in prominence versus projects that seek more functionality.

3.3   Stablecoins

While not a feature by design, the historical trading price of Bitcoin relative to fiat currencies such as the USD has been volatile. Such volatility is seen as one major barrier to the use of Bitcoin as a payment denomination. Furthermore, the transfer of fiat currencies such as USD is highly regulated. Almost all financial institutions such as banks, money transfer firms, or stock exchanges that transfer fiat money are regulated. Regulation did not keep up with the popularity of cryptocurrencies, and historically, a lot of online services where cryptocurrencies were exchanged with each other did not have the proper authorizations to deal in fiat currency.

Thus, a new breed of cryptocurrency emerged that is designed to be stable against fiat currencies. An example is Tether, which claims to maintain each token at the value of $1. Being a cryptocurrency worth $1 rather than being $1 itself, movements in Tether are not as tightly regulated as movements in the US dollar itself. Thus, users can exchange Bitcoin not into US dollars, a possibly regulated trade, but rather into Tether, an unregulated trade. Then, the Tether can be used to buy other cryptocurrencies or even be used as payment itself without having to go through the actual US dollar currency. The two other major examples are USDC and BUSD, both of which also claim to tie 1-to-1 with the US dollar. So, each USDC or BUSD is to be kept at $1.

Tether, USDC, and BUSD have managed to maintain a remarkably consistent peg to the US dollar. It is not precisely clear how they maintain their peg to the US dollar beyond a good dose of trust or acceptance by their users. To maintain their pegged values, these stablecoins all claim that they hold about $1 for every token that is circulating. There have been challenges to this, and there is no consistent audit to show that to be the case.

There is legal ambiguity on what Tether, USDC, and BUSD are doing. The pure issuing of 1-to-1 tokens for US dollars would seem unlawful without a banking license of sorts. But all three projects do not actually back each token exactly 1-to-1 with US dollars. Each rather uses some combination of other investments to mimic a 1-to-1 US dollar peg (Kharif, 2018).

Without clear auditing or other documentation of the collateral backing, these blockchain projects seem to be at high risk of fraud and collapse, as there would be tremendous incentive to create new tokens without the underlying collateral. Nonetheless, all three tokens remain highly active in use in online digital asset markets, possibly because they are intended to be only short-term intermediary holdings when trading cryptocurrencies. Thus, users are comfortable with their risk if held for only a short time.

Tether, USDC, and BUSD, as almost equivalent to digital US dollars but without corresponding regulations on their digital transfer, have unsurprisingly grown to become the 3rd, 6th, and 29th largest cryptocurrencies at the time of this writing by total value.

A more innovative version of stablecoin is known as "algorithmic stablecoins". These blockchain projects try to mimic the value of a fiat currency peg without any asset collateral at all. Instead, they try to adjust supply based on their demand to keep the price at, say, $1 per unit of cryptocurrency. They do not seem popular and whether they may actually work is unclear (Volpicelli, 2022). But algorithmic stablecoins, if they work, would be at lower risk of regulatory scrutiny compared to collateral-based stablecoins such as Tether, USDC, or BUSD.

3.4   Central Bank Digital Currencies

As a topic of discussion in relation to digital payment systems, several major central banks, such as the Bank of England, have publicly announced interest in issuing central bank digital currencies (CBDCs). The Bank of England describes such an object as:

> Central bank digital currency (CBDC) is money that a country's central bank can issue. It's called digital (or electronic) because it isn't physical money like notes and coins. It is in the form of an amount on a computer or similar device. (Bank of England [BOE], 2023)

Other countries whose central banks have announced similar interests include the USA, EU, and China. The BOE says:

> You may have heard of Bitcoin, Ether (Ethereum) and XRP. They are examples of privately issued digital assets (sometimes known as cryptocurrency or cryptoassets). CBDC are different to cryptoassets in several important ways.

> Firstly, cryptoassets are issued privately. If anything goes wrong with a cryptoasset, there's no central bank or government that can step in.

> Secondly, the value of a cryptoasset is volatile. It can go up or down quickly in a very short space of time. This isn't ideal when making payments. If we decided to issue them, digital pounds would be stable and retain their value over time. (BOE, 2023)

The seeming rationale for issuing such CBDCs is two-fold, as implied in BOE's statement above. The first is about intervention in times of crisis. The second seems to be about encouraging the use of CDBCs as a payment system in lieu of physical cash.

This stated motive can be disquieting in implication. The BOE seems to say that CBDCs may substitute for physical currency. If physical cash were to be substantially reduced or eliminated at some point, the privacy consequences to individuals could be disturbing. At the moment, the only officially authorized payment method that is not traceable is physical cash. If central banks issued CBDCs, such as the digital pound, and stopped issuing physical cash altogether, the entire official financial system would be fully under the watch and control of the central bank.

Such government-issued CBDCs are unlikely to be driven by decentralized blockchains, but even if they are, the effects would be an official loss of all formal financial privacy. Digital payment systems always leave records, even if on a blockchain. Physical cash, on the other hand, is fully untraceable.

There is evidence that physical cash, especially the $100 physical bill, is used precisely to avoid financial traceability (Judson, 2017; Wang, 2021). Speculation is that such large denominations of untraceable cash are being put to unwholesome use since most consumers do not use $100 bills in daily life. But banning physical cash in the name of countering money laundering or criminal financing needs to be balanced against some right to privacy in the financial affairs of individuals.

3.5   Digital Resource Sharing

Another category of current blockchain projects is designed for the trading of some decentralized resource, specifically some form of digital resource. This appears to be a suitable use for blockchains if the digital resource involved, which was not designed for sharing, can be in fact easily shared.

The most developed and functional examples in this category involve file storage. Examples include Storj, Siacoin, and Filecoin. The blockchains for these projects keep track of tokens that can rent the use of storage space on other people's computers. Similarly, by providing one's own extra hard disk space for others to use, one can earn these tokens (effectively renting out extra hard disk space). The files stored are encrypted. The tokens can be spent or also traded. As such, these tokens should have a clear exchange value against fiat currencies because they can be spent for disk space use, which is a service with explicit value. Additionally, these systems also provide a clear advantage for decentralization—files stored on these systems can survive the downfall of any single computer in the network. These projects combine elements of BitTorrent with blockchains.

Another example in the resource-sharing category of blockchain applications is Orchid, which gives tokens that buy the use of VPN (Virtual Private Network) bandwidth. The idea is that by allowing one's computer to be used as a VPN, one can earn Orchid coins. Similarly, Orchid coins can be spent to use someone else's computer as a VPN. Again, these tokens should have a clear exchange value since VPN provision is a valuable service to those who use it. This is a case where a clear advantage of decentralization exists, especially in regard to evading firewalls, because a different computer can provide the VPN on each use, thereby helping avoid detection. The concept of Orchid seems feasible but the technology or market, however, does not seem ready for it. It is not clear if VPN access can be technically shared easily in this way between internet users.

Yet another example is the renting out of unused graphics processing power, in a project called Rendr. In a similar fashion to Orchid, the concept seems feasible but the technology or market has not allowed it to take off, at least not as of yet.

3.6   SECURE DATA STORAGE

Much public administration, law, and finance activities in society rely on an official set of reference data that is regularly updated. There is a category of blockchain applications that imagines using blockchains to keep such data public and secure. Blockchains being public use documents that are regularly updated, such applications may fall naturally within the use of blockchains.

For example, a prominent case would be the land registry database. It is crucial that an authoritative database exists of who owns what land. Such a registry needs to be robust, accessible, and difficult to fraudulently alter. A possible way of accomplishing this, perhaps, is to put such data onto a blockchain that can be downloaded and kept up to date on any computer. Transactions can then be potentially updated between two parties without an authority that officially changes the register. Also, using decentralization would ensure the continuity of the database in case an official entity errs, collapses, gets hacked, loses data, or becomes malicious. Blockchains, being chains of provenance, will also have a full record as evidence for dispute resolution in courts or tribunals.

That was the concept behind the blockchain project known as Bitland. But that project failed, and for now, major functional blockchain projects purely to keep authoritative data in a decentralized way do not yet exist. Blockchain implementations of such projects suffer from several hindrances.

First, there may not be enough innate incentive mechanisms to encourage continuous participation by decentralized network users. It is unclear what the incentives are for someone to participate in maintaining a land registry blockchain, say, especially if they do not own land. It is difficult to create a token that aligns incentives with use. If the blockchain rewards a token for processing land transactions, it is unclear what those tokens could then be spent on. This could be a situation where altruism may come into play in the maintenance of a blockchain as a public good. It is conceivable that every landowner wishes to maintain the integrity of the land registry and thus has some incentive to contribute some resources to keeping the land registry secure. But pure altruism is often not a reliable incentive for such an important document.

Second, it is unclear what the best consensus protocol should be. For example, if there are two competing land transactions trying to get onto the blockchain, Proof-of-Work seems unlikely to be the appropriate consensus protocol for validating one over the other. Neither are other consensus rules, for example, such as taking as official the transaction with the higher transaction price. Many land transfers, such as transfer by inheritance, do not involve transaction prices. And each parcel of land being unique, transfers are often not standard. Furthermore, there are different types of interests in land that can be transferred or changed, such as complicated negotiated layers of leases and easements. A consensus protocol on how to pick between competing proposed entries is difficult to design.

Third, for very important information like land registry titles, the blockchain often must be authoritatively sanctioned in the first place. For example, the current land registration bureau of a country needs to approve a blockchain for that blockchain to gain traction. If that centralized authority withdraws approval, then the blockchain may no longer survive. Or where two authorities approve different blockchains, the very issue of legitimacy is challenged and the blockchain in itself cannot solve such a problem. To the extent that a blockchain is supposed to be free of trust in a central authority, this is often not achievable when legitimacy itself is at stake over the data.

While the incentive, consensus, and legitimacy issue for land registries can be tricky, there are situations where it could be overcome. An example of a possible application is discussed in the next chapter.

3.7   PRIVATE BLOCKCHAINS

There is arguably a category of blockchain projects where the blockchains are actually used by individuals who are already identified and known to each other, such as employees of the same company. These are sometimes called "private blockchains", where a closed network of users accesses the blockchain system.

In a conceptual sense, a blockchain is originally intended to coordinate decentralized activities by unknown or unidentified users, so while private blockchain projects may still be technically blockchain applications, it is not clear if the use of a blockchain adds any general benefit when there are more direct means of coordination and control within a closed group.

However, the use of private blockchains can sometimes solve specific information issues faced by organizations. One example of such an application is reportedly a travel health database exchange between the province of Guangdong in China and the self-governed Chinese territory of Macau (Feng, 2020). By going through a blockchain, the two territories were able to share the Covid-19 status of 17 million cross-border travelers without nominally violating local data privacy laws because they did not directly exchange the data. The blockchains in this case were not open access and were clearly under the full control of the two authorities, who were effectively the only two users, but regulation prevented them from directly exchanging and using the data. If there had been no such issue of the very specific legal situation between these two parties, they could have much more easily just emailed each other the information.

Private blockchains can thus be designed to solve very specific problems among a closed group of users. It is plausible, for example, to design blockchain mechanisms to elicit truthful data sharing among users who do not fully trust each other but need the data to cooperate. One possibly fruitful area is across complex supply chains, where detailed and accurate information sharing is critical to reduce waste throughout the entire supply chain but individual users may not fully wish to reveal their own data for competitive reasons. The current commercial solution is for supply chain partners to use a trusted third-party agent to coordinate information sharing across the supply chain but appropriately not revealing sensitive information. A carefully designed blockchain with suitable anonymity, incentives, and cryptography features can plausibly solve such sensitive scenarios. However the complexity of designing such a mechanism could be challenging. Thus, at the moment, functional blockchain solutions addressing information challenges in supply chains remain elusive.

3.8   LOYALTY TOKENS

The 4th largest cryptocurrency by market capitalization at the time of writing is known as BNB. This is a token issued by the largest cryptocurrency exchange Binance. These tokens can be used to pay transaction fees and buy services and products from Binance and some of its partners. BNB tokens are, in some sense, loyalty points. They are given as incentives to customers who signed up and traded cryptocurrencies or referred other customers to Binance. At some point, Binance also raised money by issuing BNB, an act that was later challenged as unlawful.

However, unlike typical loyalty points such as airline miles, BNB is a cryptocurrency and thus can be freely traded. Binance also has a policy of destroying certain amounts of BNB to reduce supply. The use of cryptocurrencies by single firms in this way is somewhat unprecedented. It is also unclear what the price of BNB represents. However the scale of the BNB market cap suggests that there is a good market value for this token. Very few other firms are known to have done such a thing on such a scale. This is a curious application of blockchain, and it is interesting to watch how or whether other companies may one day follow suit.

3.9   BLOCKCHAIN SCALABILITY PROJECTS

Bitcoin's processing speed and block size restrictions fundamentally restrict its widespread use as a payment system. As soon as that became clear, there was an effort to make decentralized networks such as Bitcoin faster. Usually, making blockchains faster is called the "scalability" problem.

The obvious effort to emerge was to batch Bitcoin transactions "off-chain" and then only put through the final netted Bitcoin transfers onto the official Blockchain. By netting off as many transactions as possible, a smaller number of transactions are needed on the Blockchain. For example, cryptocurrency exchanges keep track of transactions themselves until transfers onto the Blockchain are needed, batched periodically rather than continuously. Such batching efforts might even include smaller blockchains (termed "side-chains") to keep track of the batching procedures. However, any batching transfers are not official Bitcoin transactions, and any side-chains are not part of the Blockchain. Those transactions off the Blockchain are more susceptible to hacking and fraud, negating a lot of the key features of Bitcoin. (Incidentally, such batching processes can also mask and frustrate the true provenance of Bitcoin on the official Blockchain, a "mixing" procedure that can be used to reduce Bitcoin's open traceability.) These batching systems are sometimes known as "Layer 2" applications that aim to reduce the number of transactions that need to go into the limited space of blocks of the underlying "Layer 1" blockchain.

The scalability issue is sometimes expressed in terms of a "trilemma" in blockchain technologies. This trilemma refers to the notion that decentralization, scalability/speed, and security have trade-offs against each other.

The trade-offs of the trilemma are easy to see. Updating decentralized data across a diffuse base of users must by definition be slower than updating the same data on only one centralized data repository. The update needs time to propagate, all else equal. Similarly, it is almost by definition harder to update data securely across many computers as opposed to updating data securely on just one computer. Updating a diffuse network of computers leaves gaps for hackers to corrupt the update. Finally, scalability and security tend to oppose as it is, of course, easier to scale if security is compromised.

This blockchain trilemma has not been formally or technically analyzed, but it seems to be a truism that also effectively reduces to a "dilemma" rather than a "trilemma". The trilemma really only gives one discretionary dimension. The desirability of "security" and "scalability" would exist in any application—the higher the better on both, all else equal. Thus, the true decision is really on how much decentralization a particular application wants. There are intermediate degrees between the two extremes of full centralization and full decentralization, but the compromise that decentralization brings to scalability or security is an inherent one. It is not so much a problem to be solved as a trade-off to be recognized.

If being decentralized is deemed a fundamental feature of a blockchain project, then its trade-off in speed/scalability or security must be accepted rather than cured. Since security is often not to be sacrificed, many blockchain projects try to lean towards reducing decentralization to increase speed. For example, Ripple and Stellar are faster payment systems than Bitcoin, but they are both more centralized by having fewer computers that are allowed to add new blocks.

Nonetheless, there are still projects that aim to resolve all three corners of the trilemma via mechanism design or technical means. For example, the project Algorand claims to solve the trilemma using mechanism design by adopting a two-tiered consensus mechanism using random users to vote on the next block. Whether such a method is ultimately sacrificing security or decentralization is to be seen. Several other projects have sought to resolve the trilemma using various technical methods, such as "sharding", which splits up the blockchain into chunks for easier processing. It is not clear if any major project has yet to get sharding to work acceptably.

Several new, active, and prominent blockchain projects fall within the effort to make blockchains work in a scalable way. They are debated to be anything from "Layer 0", "Layer 1", and "Layer 2", to "Layer 3". There is no agreement on the layer nomenclature, but they tend to focus on a mix of scalability efforts with the added view to facilitate transactions across different blockchains. Examples include Polygon, Avalanche, Chainlink, and Polkadot. They issue tokens that seek to incentivize participation in their systems. It is not clear if any have definitively managed to resolve the trilemma.

3.10   Smart Contracts

This much more ambitious class of resource-sharing blockchain applications deserves a category and a later chapter on its own. This category refers to a range of projects with Ethereum and Solana being the largest, along with further projects driven off them. Ethereum and Solana are blockchain systems where the tokens can be exchanged for processing resources within the network. These projects envision programming capability such that they can run computer code on the blockchain, with rewards given to computers that help run the code.

This programming ability can create automatic conditional transfers of tokens in what are ambitiously termed "smart contracts". An example would be simple online gambling-like deals between any two users, where the network can compute and pay transfers according to exactly predefined rules in a game of chance. For example, a digital coin is flipped and A pays B one unit of the token if heads, otherwise B pays A one unit.

A small computational fee will be taken by the computers in the network that helped execute this small computer program.

These smart contracts do allow in theory for automatically enforceable conditional transfers of tokens between any parties in a decentralized system. It is thus conceivable that more detailed arrangements can be created, including transformational applications in the world of finance. However it seems that decentralization naturally imposes a processing capacity limit on the complexity of such programs, at least for now with the current state of the technology (Jansen et al., 2020).

A longer chapter follows on smart contracts, focusing on Ethereum and the major applications based on it.

3.11   FURTHER POTENTIAL

Academics and enthusiasts have for some time imagined all the possibilities of blockchain technology. As blockchains continue to evolve, there is palpable progress on not just the technical but also the organizational fronts.

One area that is often touted is supply chains. There is no doubt that information plays a significant role in complex supply chain networks, with corresponding issues of competitive sensitivity. Broadly, everyone can also benefit from a supply chain network with better information coordination, so there should be a good reason for blockchain applications to tackle challenges in this area.

There are also peripheral applications that surround rather than use blockchains with much potential. For example, being fully public records, the Bitcoin Blockchain can enable functions such as automatic taxation, audits, and other potential uses. There is indeed some irony that blockchain technology is now sometimes touted as a regulatory mechanism (Yermack, 2017) when Bitcoin was originally designed to elude government control.

Regardless of how blockchains are applied, failure rates of blockchain projects are high, for technological reasons but seemingly more for non-technological reasons. Over the past few years, many fortunes have been made and then quickly lost as cryptocurrencies surged and collapsed, both overall and for specific applications. Many blockchain-related companies turned out to be scams from the start or turned fraudulent later on. Other blockchain failures were well-intentioned but misconceived yet sold on to investors. Several prominent individuals of the cryptocurrency world have been sentenced to prison (e.g. BBC, 2023), died under suspicious circumstances (e.g. Vigna & Shifflett, 2019), or simply disappeared (e.g. Bartlett, 2019). Regulators around the world have been cracking down on cryptocurrencies.

Yet, few today doubt the potential of blockchain as a legitimate technology. It is correct to envision the possibilities (e.g. Chen & Bellavitis, 2020; Chen et al., 2022). The key is finding what to use it for in society. It would be incorrect to say that blockchain shall solve all the world's problems, from financial inclusion to contract disputes, from inflation to climate change. Some of the proposed or envisioned uses of blockchain are hypothetical, and some are too removed from the capabilities of secure decentralized computing as it exists today.

What is useful is a systematic framework to discuss and assess the potential of a blockchain project based on non-technical concepts and considerations of blockchain. The next chapter presents a hypothetical yet plausible blockchain application called TransChain. The chapter then following will use TransChain as an example to present a framework for assessing a blockchain project from non-technical considerations.

References

Bank of England. (2023). What is CBDC?. https://www.bankofengland.co.uk/explainers/what-is-a-central-bank-digital-currency

Bartlett, J. (2019, December 15). The £4bn OneCoin scam: How crypto-queen Dr Ruja Ignatova duped ordinary people out of billions—Then went missing. *The Times*.

BBC. (2023, September 8). Thodex cryptocurrency boss jailed for 11,196 years in Turkey for fraud. *BBC*.

Chen, Y., & Bellavitis, C. (2020). Blockchain disruption and decentralized finance: The rise of decentralized business models. *Journal of Business Venturing Insights, 13*, e00151.

Chen, Y., Lu, Y., Bulysheva, L., & Kataev, M. Y. (2022). Applications of blockchain in industry 4.0: A review. *Information Systems Frontiers*, 1–15.

Feng, C. (2020, October 22). Blockchain allowed 17 million people to travel between Guangdong, Macau amid coronavirus pandemic. *South China Morning Post*.

Jansen, M., Hdhili, F., Gouiaa, R., & Qasem, Z. (2020). Do smart contract languages need to be turing complete?. In *Blockchain and applications. Advances in intelligent systems and computing* (Vol. 1010, pp. 19–26). Springer.

Judson, R. (2017). *The death of cash? Not so fast: Demand for U.S. currency at home and abroad, 1990–2016*. International Cash Conference 2017, Deutsche Bundesbank.

Kharif, O. (2018, October 29). Stable coin backed by Circle, Coinbase draws most early demand. Bloomberg.

Vigna, P., & Shifflett, S. (2019, February 19). 'Our cash went to something': Customers hunt for bankrupt crypto exchange's missing millions. *Wall Street Journal*.

Volpicelli, G. M. (2022, May 12). Terra's crypto meltdown was inevitable. *Wired*.

Wang, J. (2021). Central banking 101. *Joseph*.

Yermack, D. (2017). Corporate governance and blockchains. *Review of Finance, 21*(1), 7–31.

CHAPTER 4

A Simple Blockchain Application

Abstract Discourse on blockchain is focused on applications with two typical features: (1) an associated cryptocurrency and (2) big impact. Neither is in fact necessary for a plausible blockchain application. This chapter presents a simple blockchain application. It is a hypothetical application called TransChain but one that might well catch on in the future. It uses no cryptocurrency. This example application will then be used to introduce the EBC Pyramid blockchain assessment framework in the next chapter.

Keywords TransChain · Blockchain application

4.1 The Problem of School Transcripts

Consider the plight of schools and universities. These institutions must keep the academic records of their students and alumni indefinitely. For those who went to the institution, such records are important in terms of formal uses such as applying for further education, seeking employment, and possibly even petitioning for immigration. It is not uncommon that transcript documents are needed decades later, and sometimes for use anywhere in the world.

S. T. Zhang, *The Potential and Limitations of Bitcoin and Ethereum*, https://doi.org/10.1007/978-3-031-56783-4_4

The authenticity of such school transcripts can be problematic. Given their importance, people may try to forge them. Some schools try to print transcripts on anti-counterfeit paper, but the standard verification method is either for schools to respond directly to queries from third parties to confirm authenticity or for the school to directly send transcripts to third parties when requested.

Such authentication requests are labor-intensive for the school. They are significant and costly functions. These are also services provided to alumni who no longer attend the school or pay tuition fees, so the costs are not borne by the users. Some schools have hired companies to handle the function. These companies often send a link to third parties so that transcripts can be downloaded from a verified source. However, third parties do not always wish to click on internet links, especially links that are not directly from the school but rather from a commercial company contracted by the school.

There is no way to authenticate transcripts if the school has lost the records. Or, most significantly, there is no way to authenticate if the school has gone defunct. While most institutions of education try to stay permanent, it is still quite common for schools to both lose records as well as go defunct.

This scenario presents a suitable application for a blockchain solution.

4.2   A BLOCKCHAIN SOLUTION—TRANSCHAIN

Consider TransChain, a hypothetical blockchain application that seeks to address the issue of academic transcript authentication. The basic blockchain solution will be an encrypted file that contains all the student transcript records from the school. This blockchain gets updated regularly by adding a new block of transcript records.

The "consensus protocol" to add new records to this blockchain is very simple. In this case, the consensus protocol is that only the school can add new blocks of records. Nobody else can. After adding each block of new records, a newly secured and encrypted blockchain file is created. As far as a school is concerned, updating is after each academic term, so maybe two or three times each year.

The latest blockchain file is kept on the school's website and anyone can freely download it and keep a copy. It is encrypted so nobody can read the file.

Each student has a record or "account" in the file that can only be decrypted with a private password. Such a password can be designed with more features. For example, there could be a personal master password to view one's transcript, from which more temporary expiring passwords can also be generated to share with third parties.

To send an authenticated version of one's transcript to a third party, the student or alumnus would send to the third party the entire blockchain file along with an expiring password to view the personal transcript. The blockchain file can be easily verified to be genuine based on usual encryption mechanisms, and hence the transcript revealed by the password is verified to be from a genuine source. The school no longer has a role after adding the records to the blockchain. The school's only responsibility in relation to transcript records is to add student records legitimately to the blockchain. Subsequent authentication can be done by the blockchain itself. The full transcript file can be distributed freely from the school's website or in a decentralized way via the network of alumni.

Eventually, if the school ceases to exist, no further transcript records will be added to the blockchain. Assume also the school's website then shuts down. The final blockchain file, as well as any earlier versions, will still exist but in a decentralized way across the alumni user base. If an alumnus needs a transcript and has not kept a copy of the blockchain file, the software can be attached to the blockchain to query for a copy of the latest blockchain file across the alumni or any network. The software can also offer a reward to the first person to send over a copy. After receiving a copy of the blockchain, the alumnus can then use it to send authenticated transcripts to third parties even when the school itself has long ceased existence.

The concept of TransChain can extend beyond schools. For example, human resource records can be kept on such a system so that ex-employees can have an authenticated record of their employment if and when such evidence is called for, even after the demise of the company.

4.3   EVALUATION OF TRANSCHAIN

The key question is whether TransChain is a good blockchain application. Does it make sense? Is it likely to work?

To answer these questions and examine the viability of TransChain, there needs to be a framework of the key considerations. The next chapter presents a framework for such an analysis called the EBC Pyramid.

CHAPTER 5

The EBC Pyramid Framework

Abstract This chapter presents a framework of key considerations in the assessment of potential blockchain projects such as the hypothetical TransChain.

Keywords EBC Pyramid · Economic Layer · Blockchain Layer · Competitive Layer · Incentives

5.1 The Need for a Framework

Bitcoin, for historical reasons, grew from technical circles. However, the innovation is more organizational than technical. Bitcoin used established technologies and organized them in a way to align user incentives so that a blockchain document could be maintained officially for a common purpose.

Many blockchain projects have since sought to innovate on the "technology" but gave much less thought to the non-technical considerations of the blockchain projects, often changing little from the basic Bitcoin organizational setup. For example, Litecoin, once deemed as the "silver" to Bitcoin's "gold", is organizationally identical to Bitcoin. Litecoin has some differences from Bitcoin in the technical parameters, but it is organizationally the same.

© The Author(s), under exclusive license to Springer Nature   43
Switzerland AG 2024
S. T. Zhang, *The Potential and Limitations of Bitcoin and Ethereum*,
https://doi.org/10.1007/978-3-031-56783-4_5

It can be imagined that Litecoin was created with a technical focus. From that angle, Litecoin is faster than Bitcoin, and its parameters are such that it has a lower transaction fee. While those are technological improvements, from a non-technical angle, Litecoin adds very little value over Bitcoin. From the non-technical perspective, Litecoin is not a promising project in light of the existence of Bitcoin.

The EBC Pyramid is a framework to highlight the non-technical considerations that blockchain projects need to be filtered and questioned on. This is not a definitive framework, and individual blockchain projects will have their own merits. But without due regard to the three key layers of the EBC Pyramid, a blockchain project may simply not make enough sense to have potential on non-technical considerations.

For a blockchain project, the three non-technical layers to consider are the Economic Layer, the Blockchain Layer, and the Competitive Layer. A project may very well have weaknesses in one or more of the three layers. But there should be sufficient merit in each of these non-technical areas for a blockchain project to have overall potential.

The EBC Pyramid asks two key questions in each layer. These are matters that should be given serious consideration. The EBC Pyramid is shown in Fig. 5.1. The questions are not exhaustive but are key to assessing blockchain projects.

This chapter discusses these three layers further and sometimes refers to TransChain as the demonstrative example.

5.2   The Economic Layer

Since Bitcoin, blockchain projects have proliferated. They cover a diverse range of topics and intended applications. They often borderline on speculative or hypothetical use cases, and sometimes even the fantastical.

As far as the non-technical perspective is concerned, blockchain is simply software. And all software should begin by addressing a current economic need. Software has no use addressing a technical point for its own sake. There should be some real economic issue at play for the software to be used on. The two questions to be considered for the Economic Layer are:

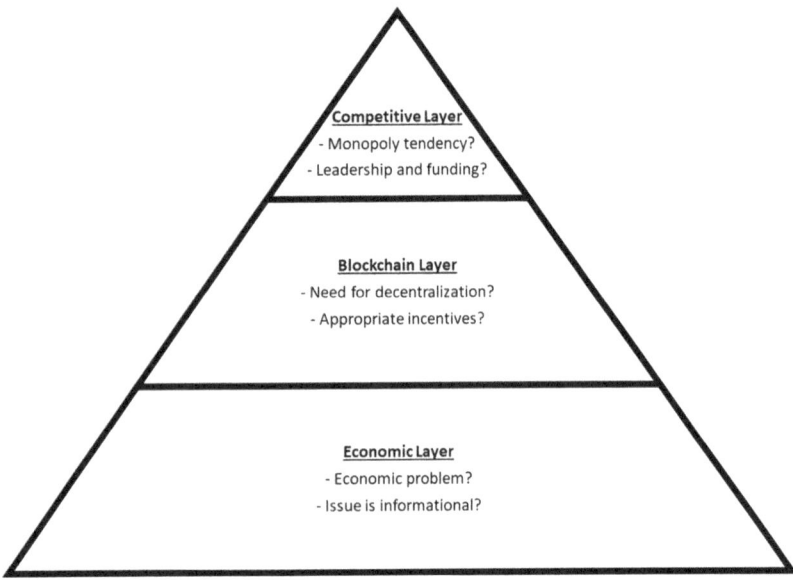

Fig. 5.1 The EBC pyramid (*Source* Author)

5.2.1   Is There a Real Economic Need?

While potential or speculative economic needs can be plausible grounds for a blockchain application, projects driven by speculative economic needs are less likely to work. The project should address economic problems that are as immediate as possible. The economic problem may not be large. It could be modest. But it should be current. If there is no current problem to solve, the practicality is that there is likely to be no immediate users.

Related to this question of economic need is whether the existing solution, if one exists, has some defect that this project can fix. Sometimes, there is already an incumbent solution that solves the economic need. If there is nothing wrong with the incumbent, there is unlikely to be a current economic need for a blockchain project to address the same issue. However, if the incumbent solution is defective, costly, or undesirable, then a genuine need exists for a new solution. Should a blockchain solution be better, cheaper, or desirable, then the economic basis is established.

Referring back to TransChain, there is a possibly wasteful process in the existing system. That is, there is an inefficient use of resources in authenticating a transcript that has already been provided repeatedly in the last for almost every student or alumnus. Third parties are running a double check on the authenticity of transcripts, and this leads to diverse requests to the school records office from all around the world. There is an actual cost to the manpower used to deal with what is a very routine task. Furthermore, the existing process lacks the feature of continuity if the school is ever to shut down. Therefore, there is a plausible current economic basis to TransChain.

5.2.2   Is the Issue One of Information?

Simply having an economic need is still not enough in the consideration of the Economic Layer. Blockchain, being software, can only really address issues that are fundamentally informational in nature. That is, blockchain is most suited for problems such as record-keeping, coordination, paperwork, and information sharing. Blockchain can address information-related matters such as authentication, privacy, and security.

Blockchain has relatively little direct application to physical products or services. There are, for example, somewhat misguided applications of blockchain in physically tracking the sale of goods. Even if one were to label physical products with barcodes that link to a blockchain, such labels can simply be peeled off to circumvent the system. While blockchains can be plausible in applications, say, where passwords to computer systems are kept on a blockchain so that only certain users can have access, blockchains still cannot prevent the computer hardware from being physically damaged or taken away.

Thus, in the assessment of a blockchain application, it is important to consider whether the fundamental issue to be solved is both economically relevant and also is one related to information. In the example TransChain, authenticating transcripts is clearly a case related to information, and thus it is a plausible use of a blockchain.

5.3   THE BLOCKCHAIN LAYER

Not every problem should or even can be solved by a blockchain solution. Many can simply be solved by regular software or some type of business service. There are questions to ask if the existing economic problem is indeed suitable for a blockchain solution.

5.3.1   *Is There a Fundamental Need for Decentralization to Justify Trade-offs?*

The central motivation of blockchain applications is decentralization. If not for at least some need for decentralization, there is no purpose in considering blockchain as a solution. Blockchains are capacity-constrained, slow, and redundant software systems. Without some fundamental need for decentralization, there is no good reason to use blockchains to address an identified issue.

The need for decentralization can be various. But usually, the users are diffuse, uncoordinated, and unascertainable, while central administrative control is relatively weak, deliberately or by accident rather than intent. For example, the motivation could be due to difficulty in finding a reliable person or entity to run the system. Or if any central administrator would be too transient to be effective, and the system needs to outlast them. It could be even that it is not clear who is in charge, as in situations of political or economic upheaval. There may also be a deliberate avoidance of a central authority on matter of principle. Or that the data contained in the blockchain are of such long-term importance that they must be kept in a highly redundant fashion outside the control of any single entity.

Decentralization will necessarily involve a trade-off in scalability or security in a software system. Thus, if a motivation for decentralization cannot be clearly expressed, there are likely more scalable and secure solutions that will solve the problem without blockchains. It would be hard to argue how the hassle of a decentralized blockchain can be justified.

In a private company, for example, there are far more effective and efficient ways to coordinate any activity of current employees than via a blockchain. So, intra-company issues relating to employee coordination are unlikely to be good candidates for blockchains. Current employees are subject to centralized control and contact, so they can be given instructions directly. Furthermore, there is an ascertainable list of employees. If there is such a list, one can simply email them because their identities and roles are known. Even if some type of interaction is desired between the employees, there are existing software solutions such as discussion boards, chat channels, and other collaboration tools that are far more effective than a blockchain at achieving any collaborative group goal. Blockchains are often not the most efficient way to organize a known and stable group of users.

However, consider how this is different for TransChain. The alumni of a school are far more diffuse, uncoordinated, and unascertainable. The school cannot easily reach out to all their alumni. Many of the alumni would have moved, passed, or otherwise become untraceable. Nor do most alumni usually have active interest in dealing with their alma mater. The alumni users shall be emerging from the woods to reach out to the school only when and if they need transcripts. Thus, there is no practical and direct way for the school or indeed anyone appointed by the school such as an alumni coordinator to reach out to the users to actively coordinate anything. This situation thus makes a suitable case for a decentralized blockchain solution where users can just go to the public blockchain when needed without the school having to actively deal with the alumni pool.

Furthermore, the reliability in having school transcripts authenticated is far more important than speed or scalability concerns. Thus, for TransChain, any drawbacks in speed or scalability are acceptable trade-offs in light of the rationale for decentralization.

5.3.2   Is There Incentive for Users to Contribute for the Benefit of the Whole?

The biggest lacuna for a decentralized blockchain system to function is that individual users are not incentivized to keep the system alive as a whole. Or, if they do have incentive, those incentives are not aligned or sufficient. Therefore, some individual incentive or benefit is crucial for users to help contribute to the system. Furthermore, such incentives need to be carefully designed to be both sufficient and aligned to the overall goals of the blockchain system.

The incentive in this context does not directly relate to the incentive to corrupt the blockchain. Typically, users of blockchains do wish to corrupt the blockchain for own benefit. For example, TransChain users will wish to change their own transcripts to reflect better school marks, and Bitcoin users will wish to send all Bitcoin to their own account. These concerns of the blockchain are secured by cryptography, not by incentives.

The incentives relate to user participation. Cryptography does not secure user participation. User participation needs to be secured by proper incentive design.

Most blockchain systems at the moment issue cryptocurrencies to incentivize user participation. The system incentivizes users by awarding an associated cryptocurrency as a participation reward, such as the mining feature of Bitcoin. Such a cryptocurrency reward, if it has value, can secure user participation. Value of the cryptocurrency can be derived from some actual use for the token, such as being spendable to run processing on the blockchain or to rent disk space from other users, or by somehow having an established market value for its resale.

Cryptocurrency rewards from the blockchain itself, however, are not the only way to set up incentives for user participation. With some thinking, participation can sometimes be secured by the use of the blockchain itself. In the case of TransChain, for example, each school alumnus is incentivized to keep a copy of their own transcripts for their own use. Assuming the whole file with everyone's transcripts is not too large, alumni are not overly burdened by storing a copy of the entire file for their own use. As long as each individual person has an incentive to keep a copy of their own transcript, they will automatically keep the transcript of everyone else who came before him or her. Thus, personal incentive alone in the case of TransChain serves to secure participation in the system.

It is also not needed for participation incentives to be issued out of the same blockchain as a cryptocurrency. There is nothing preventing any type of payment as a reward to those who participate in a blockchain. For example, TransChain can easily be set up to charge a fee to anyone who sends out the latest blockchain in response to a request. Such a fee can be done in Bitcoin or another established cryptocurrency. TransChain does not need to issue its own cryptocurrency to have an incentive. In fact, it is foreseeable that a number of future blockchain applications will use cross-chain smart contracts to make incentive payments in established cryptocurrencies such as Bitcoin or Ethereum rather than issue their own cryptocurrencies to incentivize participation.

Thus, proper user incentive schemes are crucial for blockchain projects. This aspect is core. Incentives can take on a variety of forms, be intrinsic or extrinsic, and need not affect every single user all the time. But the incentives need to make sense for the blockchain to function, and they need to align with the purpose of the blockchain.

5.4   THE COMPETITIVE LAYER

Blockchain applications, like any other service provider, will have competition. If all other matters seem satisfactory, the next questions to consider in the context of a blockchain project are related to competitors that seek to do the same thing. In this area, blockchain competition has unique characteristics versus traditional businesses.

Because blockchains are decentralized, they are also typically open-source in their software. Thus, all their underlying workings are open. This poses a problem because it is easy for a competitor blockchain project to simply replicate the system. Blockchain systems can be copied and pasted.

As such, blockchain projects can face stiff competition from very similar blockchains in addition to non-blockchain solutions to address the same problems. The competition dynamics can be difficult, and there are few strategic options for maneuver.

The two key competitive considerations for a given blockchain project relate to natural monopolization and sustainable governance.

5.4.1   Is There a Natural Monopoly Effect in the System?

Blockchains that address similar issues lack very clear differentiation from each other. Differentiation is key to traditional business competition. But differentiation is difficult to maintain for blockchains if they can be copied so easily. So, the only real strategy for a blockchain project against competitors addressing the same issue is to seek a monopoly.

The best scenario is to assess whether a given blockchain naturally tends towards a monopoly. This is a slightly different style of monopoly from traditional businesses. A blockchain monopoly is where a single blockchain system dominates the field, but yet the system itself has at least some measure of decentralization over its users.

There are several ways that a blockchain project can have monopoly tendencies.

One way a blockchain can gain a natural monopoly is by having a network effect. That is, where users use the blockchain to interact with each other. The more existing users there are in one specific project, the more valuable that project becomes to attract further users seeking to interact with the existing users. The nature of network effects is that one project becomes the natural monopoly; usually, this is the biggest project at any time. It is very difficult to dislodge the largest project from its leading position when there are network effects.

The nature of Bitcoin, for example, lends itself well to network effects. Because users can only send Bitcoin to others in the Bitcoin network, the more users there are already, the more attractive the entire Bitcoin network becomes because more people can readily send and receive Bitcoin than in some other payment token. To compete Bitcoin out of such a leading position would be exceptionally difficult. A new user would find fewer counterparties to transact with on a smaller network such as Litecoin, but on Bitcoin, there would be very many counterparties. Thus, Bitcoin dominates the payment system. It is the largest. And the largest tends to attract even more users versus competitors. Among pure payment systems, Bitcoin is likely to only get bigger.

Related to network effects is the notion of longevity and authority. In applications that rely on using blockchains as a means of storing data, there is very little defense against a competitor that decides to store the same data on a competing blockchain. In fact, the competitor can simply just fork the existing blockchain.

In such circumstances, the major competitive angle is longevity or some other indication of authority. Again, these are sources of natural monopolization. All else equal, the longest-existing blockchain to address an issue would be taken to be the original and most authoritative. Thus, in such applications, being the first-mover has particular advantage in having the authority of history that other projects cannot claim.

Authority can also arise from the initial backing of an authority. For example, in TransChain, each school would set up their own official blockchain using the TransChain system. This initial setup by the school authority will remain, even if the school later drops away from the picture. Any unauthorized blockchains for a school's transcripts are unlikely to win users over the TransChain blockchain. TransChain thus has monopoly strength. In blockchain applications, it is important to pick the most authoritative project, however derived, as other competitors would find it difficult to compete against the authoritative blockchain. It may be ironic, but longevity and authority can matter in blockchains.

5.4.2 Is There Viable Long-term Governance and Funding?

The formal analysis of collective decision-making is depressing for democracy as a way to govern. The Arrow Impossibility Theorem (Arrow, 1950) shows that under a set of reasonable assumptions, there is no collective decision-making mechanism that avoids a dictatorship. Generally, true decentralization is not stable or effective. Not only do actors try to take control of the system, but larger participants are given more voting weight in blockchain democracy systems, tending to concentrate influence over time.

What this means in practice is that blockchain projects, rather than being fully decentralized, tend to have some type of leadership. Oftentimes, this leadership comes from the founders of the blockchain project. Such leadership is needed to drive the blockchain project. It is unlikely that a fully decentralized group of users can muster the direction, will, and resources to make any progress. It is likely that users will get stuck in the decision-making, as Arrow (1950) would predict.

This practical need for leadership is at odds with the ideology of a decentralized system. However, the paradox of voting is real, where self-interested participants will not find the costs of voting to outweigh the benefits. Without some active leadership, blockchain systems will struggle to get off the ground. There will be degrees of decentralization, but a blockchain project with full decentralization is unlikely to progress without leadership.

However, leaders are not dictators, and blockchain-based systems cannot have dictators in the same sense as countries or companies might. Any project based on a public blockchain can fork and leave bad leadership behind. Thus, as long as the core of a blockchain system is open and public, leaders are not fully in control. The open-source code of the system prevents abuse, and there is an infinite backup system on the blockchain to roll back any unpopular changes made by leaders.

These considerations lead to the assessment of the governance and leadership of any particular blockchain project. Blockchain leaders, because they are necessary to advance the project, cannot survive on fans alone. There needs to be some form of business model so that the leaders, marketers, and developers of the code can get income for their work.

In the early era of blockchain, projects funded themselves by selling their own cryptocurrencies in Initial Coin Offerings ("ICOs"). The early waves of blockchain meant that projects often raised substantial amounts of funds based on little more than a conceptual "whitepaper" and a website. Many of the early blockchain projects sought to fund themselves on the assumption of rising prices for their own cryptocurrencies, a portion of which they would reserve for themselves for gradual sale over time. Blockchain promoters would also even pay employees at least partly in their own cryptocurrency, in a modern parallel to employee stock options. Sure enough, some of these blockchain ICOs turned out to be scams, and regulators began to crack down. But as the field matured, blockchain projects became more organized and even tap into traditional financing such as venture capital.

These all point to the need for some type of business model or plan to give the leaders of the project a way to fund themselves. Even if the motive of a blockchain project is not maximum profit to the leaders, there needs to be a viable plan to fund those who are leading the project, at least for as long as they have sufficient user support.

Leadership structure is in the top layer of the EBC Pyramid, because competitiveness as a blockchain project needs a sustainable long-term business model to fund project leadership. Such governance plans would also consider how the leadership changes over time. The business model is not going to be consistent across the wide variety of blockchain applications. But the assessment of blockchain projects needs to give crucial consideration to who is going to lead the project and how they are to be paid. The question is whether the leadership and funding arrangements are strong and sustainable.

The TransChain project, for example, has a simple funding proposal. Such a project would be funded by the school for as long as possible. If the school shuts, the database is not expected to change further but would remain available for as long as possible unless another leader emerges to advance it in some way. In the context of school alumni, it is possible that volunteers can maintain the project if the school ceases to exist.

In the context of commercial blockchain endeavors, funding for the leaders is likely to be a service fee or tax on the users. However, due to the recency of blockchains, no project at the moment has a detailed succession plan on how new leaders can take charge and be funded. This is an area where the best competitive strategy is yet to be written.

5.5 Evaluating TransChain Through the EBC Pyramid

The EBC Pyramid in this chapter is set up as a pyramid. That is, there is a hierarchy of importance. Having upper layers without equally or stronger lower layers is unstable. The outcome of the project would be uncertain until the lower layers are clear.

TransChain, if it existed, would seem to have a fairly solid case at the bottom. It is addressing a current economic problem in a better way than the existing solution. A blockchain approach seems applicable due to the nature of the users, and the users are plausibly incentivized. Competition from other blockchains is unlikely if the school authorizes one particular blockchain based on TransChain, and there is a possible plan to fund the project for as long as possible.

Certainly, depending on the facts, many other considerations can make or break a particular blockchain project. However, the EBC Pyramid would be a good starting point to pick out key strengths or weaknesses in a blockchain project. If one were to start a business to help schools set up TransChain systems, the EBC Pyramid seems to conclude that it would be a reasonably good pursuit.

The next two chapters revisit Bitcoin and Ethereum in light of the EBC Pyramid.

Reference

Arrow, K. (1950). A difficulty in the concept of social welfare. *Journal of Political Economy, 58*(4), 328–346.

CHAPTER 6

Revisiting Bitcoin with the EBC Pyramid

Abstract This chapter returns to a more in-depth discussion of Bitcoin in light of its mechanisms and the EBC Pyramid. There is significant debate on what gives Bitcoin its value, and the main arguments are examined in this chapter. This discussion necessarily involves some discussion of the monetary system.

Keywords Inflation · Gold · Money supply

6.1 The Economic Layer of Bitcoin

Among all the blockchain projects, Bitcoin is the most valuable, with a total market value over US\$ 500 billion. Indeed, that figure exceeds the value of outstanding physical currency and coins of most countries except the USA. As a blockchain success story, it can be argued that Bitcoin might score quite well on the considerations of the EBC Pyramid.

However, Bitcoin is not perfect. In fact, the biggest uncertainty and probably the subject of most debate is whether Bitcoin has a clear economic basis to satisfy the Economic Layer. Fundamentally, does Bitcoin solve any current economic problem?

There is substantial popular and academic debate on the exact economic basis of Bitcoin. As the fundamental layer of the EBC Pyramid,

S. T. Zhang, *The Potential and Limitations of Bitcoin and Ethereum*, https://Doi.org/10.1007/978-3-031-56783-4_6

55

this debate requires attention to conclude if Bitcoin is ultimately a good project.

There is the conception of Bitcoin as a replacement for money itself. The use of money is typically expressed as three-fold: as a unit of account, as a medium of exchange, and as a store of value. Other observers such as Yermack (2013) have looked at the volatility, correlation, and adoption of Bitcoin in their time to conclude that Bitcoin is a poor substitute for money. This discussion offers a slightly different angle.

Bitcoin's use as a unit of account is not plausible as the economic basis to use Bitcoin as money. There has never been a plausible economic problem before Bitcoin that the world needed to find a unit of account over the internet. Even if the digital world did have such an economic issue, anything such as the US dollar would work just as well as any other unit of account, and an entire Bitcoin system to serve as a unit of account would be vastly superfluous.

The initial intended function of Bitcoin was as a *payment system*, that is, as a medium of exchange. Bitcoin has been loosely described as such in general, including in this book. More specifically, Bitcoin was started to be a system for making small payments online (Nakamoto, 2008). As far as small online payments go, though, Bitcoin did not solve the problem well. While there might have been an economic problem with making small payments online, Bitcoin is not a solution. Bitcoin's capacity is too constrained to be used for regular small online payments in any convenient way.

But on a bigger scale, the economic basis of Bitcoin often cited is that fiat money can be created at will and thus be inflated by a central bank arbitrarily. Bitcoin, it is argued, cannot be created at will and thus cannot be eroded arbitrarily due to inflation. This issue of countering inflation, then, is the supposed solution of Bitcoin over the perceived problem of inflation in fiat currency.

Is inflation a problem in the existing monetary system? And if so, does Bitcoin solve the problem? This line of logic deserves some consideration.

6.2   Money and Inflation

It is plausible for something like Bitcoin to be used as money as a medium of exchange, despite its shortcomings. Indeed, almost anything could serve such purpose. Modern money is fully based on imagination. Modern money as fiat currency is little more than holding up a piece of paper and saying it is worth whatever number is written on it. Thus, the use of Bitcoin for such purpose is within reason.

To think about this, there is a basic formula in macroeconomics:

$$MV = PQ$$

M is money supply. V is the "velocity" of money. P is the general price level. Q is the quantity of goods and services produced.

The right-hand side of this equation is the nominal GDP of an economy per year. It is the average price of all goods and services produced P, multiplied by the quantity of all goods and services produced Q. The arithmetic would be approximate in practice, but the concept is not controversial. It is simply price multiplied by quantity.

The left-hand side of this equation has M, the money supply available, multiplied by a "velocity" V, which is how many times in a year one unit of the money got spent.

Say there were 250 units of goods and services produced. Average price was $40 each. The GDP would be $40 × 250 = $10,000. This $10,000 in GDP transactions could have been done with a money supply of $1000 worth of currency in circulation with each dollar transacting an average of 10 times over the year. Or it could be done with a money supply of $2000 worth of currency in circulation with each dollar transacting an average of 5 times over the year.

The amount of currency in circulation ($1000 or $2000 in above example) is the money supply M. The number of times it transacts per year on average (10 or 5 in above example) is called the "velocity" of that currency V.

The equation MV = PQ is by definition true. Thus, it is not controversial. What is not so clear is how these variables move, because none of these variables are under the direct control of the government. The only variable that might be influenced by the government is the money supply M.

So, if V stays the same, increasing money supply M could increase price P or output Q or some combination of both. If only price P increased to match an increase in M, all the increase went into inflation. If only quantity Q increased to match an increase in M, it would all go into output growth. Often, P and Q might increase together when M is increased.

Before it actually happens, it is not at all clear how much increase will go into P and how much will go into Q. The result ultimately depends on the supply capacity of the economy. If supply is already at capacity, any increase will go into price P without affecting output. If there is a lot of excess capacity, a lot of the increase may go into quantity Q.

There is the complication of V. Increasing M may be accompanied by a decrease in V, in which case there can be no effect or even negative effect on the GDP. During the 2007–2008 Financial Crisis, central banks wanted to increase M to get output growth and inflation, but V instead dramatically dropped, leading to low inflation along with modest output growth (Wen & Arias, 2014). It did not lead to increased inflation for over a decade as many people feared despite the seemingly large money supply in circulation. In actuality, some inflation was the intention, but it did not happen due to large decreases in V.

There is furthermore the complication that M is only influenced but not directly under the control of the central bank. Thus, even if the central bank wanted to encourage money supply growth, it may not happen. This is because a substantial part of money supply is driven by private commercial lending and the central bank can only encourage rather than directly control such lending.[1]

6.3   Bitcoin and Inflation

One of the presumed benefits of Bitcoin is that it restricts the central bank from arbitrarily influencing money supply M. Consider an economy fully denominated in Bitcoin. The same equation applies.

$$MV = PQ$$

For Bitcoin, M is capped. The supply of Bitcoin cannot exceed 21 million. Furthermore, and crucially, V is also capped for Bitcoin. This is because there is a block size limit on how many transactions are allowed every 10 minutes. Velocity of Bitcoin is capped.

Thus, if Bitcoin is to be used in the economy as a medium of exchange, the left-hand side of the equation is effectively constant. It cannot grow beyond a certain point. If anything, it may even decrease as people lose their passwords and Bitcoins are lost.

In this scenario, if the economy is to grow in output Q, the price level P must decrease to balance the left-hand side. Therefore, the Bitcoin system

---

[1] In brief, increased lending by private commercial banks increases the money supply.

is *deflationary*. Deflation means each unit of Bitcoin will trade for more and more output rather than less and less. Each Bitcoin will be worth more in real terms.

Appreciating Bitcoin value may seem good to those who have some. But deflationary monetary systems like that do not sustain.

Deflation in money in an economy is painful. During deflation, the purchasing power of money increases over time. Therefore, people do not spend. People prefer to save. Without growth in spending, there is no growth in output. This then has the circular effect of keeping the economy in a depression with lower and lower output as people keep hoarding the money as an investment in itself. Furthermore, when money deflates, those who owe debt, including the government, have an increasingly heavy burden as the money they owe increases in purchasing power over time and becomes increasingly harder to pay back. Knowing this, people also do not borrow to invest in actual economic capacity expansion, further reducing activity in the system. It is hard to get out of deflation.

Because deflation is worse than inflation, the official target of most central banks in the developed economies is to keep money inflation around 2–3%. This is meant to keep a safe distance from accidentally falling into deflation while still keeping inflation low. The increase in monetary supply after the Financial Crisis of 2007–2008 was *intended* to create inflation so as not to fall into deflation and depression. But it did not, in fact, happen.

It can then be seen that the Bitcoin economy is not a cure for inflation. It is, in fact, something worse than inflation. It is deflation, instead. The world has not yet seen a positive or sustainable monetary ending to an economy in deflation. What will eventually happen in the Bitcoin economy is that Q will begin to drop as nobody spends Bitcoin. This will ultimately limit the use of Bitcoin as a viable form of money.

This analysis shows that Bitcoin is unsuitable as a replacement for fiat money in terms of medium of exchange. Because Bitcoin is deflationary and such monetary systems do not work if economies are to grow.

6.4   Bitcoin as an Asset

The unsuitability of gold as a payment system does not mean gold itself is worthless. Very much the opposite, gold is valuable even when not used in the context of a payment system. The same argument has been advanced for Bitcoin. Indeed, an alternative theory of how Bitcoin's value derives from its capped supply is via analogy to gold.

That is, Bitcoin may be used as a store of value, the third and final use for money. In many ways, gold and Bitcoin share a lot of characteristics. Both have limited supply, low transaction volumes, meaningful transaction costs and delays, relatively volatile value, and some storage costs.

If Bitcoin's economic basis is to be based on gold, the first key question under the EBC Pyramid is then whether there is a current problem to be solved in relation to gold. The possible answer would be that gold has the problem of being physically heavy and unwieldly to handle. The advantage of Bitcoin is that it is far more convenient than gold to keep and use. This is a plausible logic.

If Bitcoin were a digital record of actual gold ownership, and owner-ship of actual gold had been somehow hard to show or keep track of, then Bitcoin might have more merit in the Economic Layer. But that is not the problem with physical gold, and Bitcoin falls somewhat short of addressing the physical inconvenience of gold. The reason is that the physical shortcomings of gold are not informational in nature. Thus, regardless of how hard Bitcoin tries, it cannot fundamentally address gold's physical problems. Bitcoin can appear to solve the problem by analogy, but analogies are not actual solutions.

There is, in fact, no natural relationship between gold and Bitcoin other than by analogy. And analogies are not inventions that can solve the original problem.

Consider if Bitcoin were not named Bitcoin and given the framing of a bullion financial system with mining and exchanges. Consider instead if the system had been called Bit-Points or Gift-Tokens, and given a frame-work of virtual valentine cards being sent between players in an online dating game. Then any analogy between such points and physical gold would be quite fantastical.

The reason for the analogy is likely the belief that gold gets its value by convention or trust, as does Bitcoin. But that notion is not correct for gold. Fiat currency gets its value by convention or trust. Gold is the opposite to fiat currency in this regard. Gold is a physical substance whose rarity does not need collective acceptance to be true. But fiat currency is an artificial object whose rarity of supply is accepted by convention. Bitcoin can be similar to gold or to fiat currency, but not to both at the same time. It would be fiat currency that Bitcoin fundamentally shares more in common with, not gold. Just like fiat currency, Bitcoin's rarity of supply is limited by convention rather than by physical impossibility.

Thus, the analogy of Bitcoin to gold would seem to be misconceived, and the idea that Bitcoin solves some economic problem of physical gold is not a plausible economic basis. To the extent that money is a store for value, then, Bitcoin is also on uncertain ground.

The Economic Layer of Bitcoin, in sum, is not clear on its merits. It is still plausible that Bitcoin functions as some hybrid store of value operating in between fiat money and gold, but it is not fully clear if there ever was an economic problem that fell into that space.

6.5   THE BLOCKCHAIN LAYER OF BITCOIN

Assuming that Bitcoin does have a solid Economic Layer, the next layer is the Blockchain Layer of the EBC Pyramid. This seems much clearer in the case of Bitcoin.

As far as the Blockchain Layer is concerned, users of Bitcoin are numerous, and not ascertained. The initial as well as the subsequent goals of Bitcoin include the ability of strangers to transact online without a trusted intermediary. Thus, the need for a decentralized system is fundamental to the system. There is a weakness in that Bitcoin has restricted scalability. It is slow and transaction capacity is limited. But this is a trade-off that must be accepted if decentralization is key, which it is for Bitcoin.

Furthermore, in the Blockchain Layer, the participation incentives of Bitcoin via mining tournaments are established and seem to have worked for over a decade in maintaining the system. The personal incentives of miners align with the whole system.

Thus, the Blockchain Layer is on fairly solid ground in respect to Bitcoin, assuming the Economic Layer is stable.

6.6   THE COMPETITIVE LAYER OF BITCOIN

On the Competitive Layer, Bitcoin is a network system with transactions between users. This is a classic example of a natural monopoly via network effects. The bigger the Bitcoin network, the easier it is to find a counterparty in the network to transact with. Thus, transactions done in cryptocurrency should ultimately coalesce onto one system that all counterparties agree to use. Among blockchains, Bitcoin was the first and has the longest tenure, giving Bitcoin the highest recognition and legitimacy that no other blockchain can compete on. Thus, Bitcoin is expected to continue its dominance of payment in cryptocurrencies as the standard-bearer of payments. It would be difficult for a competitor to displace Bitcoin from its dominance in this regard, and Bitcoin is competitively well-positioned.

Bitcoin is shakier on its funding and leadership model. There is no clear plan on funding or leadership. A relatively small number of active developers are responsible for maintaining the most important aspects of the Bitcoin system. These developers are funded by a small group of commercial and non-profit entities, including MIT (Mochari, 2016). Satoshi Nakamoto never set up a governance or funding model for the software development of Bitcoin, and thus this is one of the key areas that the Bitcoin system needs to collectively address eventually. For current purposes, this may not be a pressing issue because Bitcoin's leadership and funding are no worse than any other blockchain system.

Thus, overall on the Competitive Layer, Bitcoin seems to be established fairly well relative to any competitors.

6.7   BITCOIN AND THE EBC PYRAMID

In conclusion, Bitcoin seems to be a solid application of blockchain according to the EBC Pyramid, with the crucial and important exception that its Economic Layer is not immediately clear, at least not on a grand scale. The paradigm-shaking potential use of Bitcoin as a replacement for money does not seem to stand up to detailed scrutiny.

Given the large market value of Bitcoin, it is possible that there is an economic basis for Bitcoin that the market has recognized but nobody has yet prominently explained or clarified. Alternatively, the economic basis of Bitcoin may be driven on mistaken beliefs about what economic problems Bitcoin can address.

REFERENCES

Mochari, I. (2016, March 29). MIT announces $900,000 Bitcoin developer fund. *Inc.*

Nakamoto, S. (2008). *Bitcoin: A peer-to-peer electronic cash system.* Retrieved January 31, 2018, from www.bitcoin.org

Wen, Y., & Arias, M. A. (2014, September 1). What does money velocity tell us about low inflation in the US?. *Federal Reserve Bank.*

Yermack, D. (2013). *Is Bitcoin a real currency? An economic appraisal* (No. w19747). National Bureau of Economic Research.

CHAPTER 7

Ethereum and the EBC Pyramid

Abstract This chapter turns to a more in-depth discussion of Ethereum and smart contracts in light of the EBC Pyramid. The nature and potential of smart contracts are discussed along with some of its prominent possible applications.

Keywords Ethereum · Smart contract · Prediction market · Decentralized Autonomous Organization · Non-Fungible Token

7.1 THE ADVENT OF ETHEREUM

It is quite remarkable that Bitcoin worked. However, its functionality is minimal. Shortly after Bitcoin, Ethereum started with the far more ambitious goal of allowing for conditional transactions on a blockchain. That is, Ethereum shall be a blockchain that can also run computer programs. These programs can, for example, send transactions at a certain time in the future or conditional on the outcome of a random number generator, or on conditions such as seeing a trigger transaction occur elsewhere on the blockchain. Ethereum's programming functionality in theory has the capability to be complex, but in reality, the programs so far have been fairly simple (Jansen et al., 2020).

S. T. Zhang, *The Potential and Limitations of Bitcoin and Ethereum*, https://doi.org/10.1007/978-3-031-56783-4_7

The mechanics of running computer programs in a decentralized way is not straightforward. But the concept used in Ethereum was inspired by Bitcoin. Those who wish to run a program will need to offer a fee (called "gas") that would be paid to users who run each operational step of the program. The token in Ethereum is called Ether, which is the cryptocurrency that gas is paid in. Ether otherwise also functions like Bitcoin with balances that are kept track of on the Ethereum blockchain. The programming language used on Ethereum is called Solidity. There have since been other blockchains such as Solana that have programming ability. A decentralized blockchain-based computer program is often called a "smart contract".

7.2   The Economic Layer of Ethereum and Smart Contracts

The key functionality of Ethereum is the smart contract. The word "smart contract" is confusing nomenclature for a computer program, because the word or concept of a contract is not typical in such contexts. But some of the fundamental purposes of decentralized blockchain programming involve transactions between different accounts on the blockchain, which can plausibly be called contracts.

One simple example of such a program can be the following. If in 24 hours, 1 Bitcoin has been transferred into a particular Bitcoin address, then 10 Ether shall be transferred from one Ether address to another Ether address.

The key detail of such a program is that if this program is written into the Ethereum blockchain in suitable Solidity code, it is publicly seen and it will run on the blockchain. Importantly, such a program will be run by a decentralized network of mining computers.[1] As such, unlike traditional computer programs, nobody can stop this program from running once it is started (assuming it was given enough gas).

This particular computer program seems to be a trade of 1 Bitcoin for 10 Ether. There are a couple of points to notice about this trade if it is written into the Ethereum blockchain.

[1] Ethereum initially used a Proof-of-Work consensus protocol to mine. It changed to a Proof-of-Stake consensus protocol on 15 September 2022. Thus, Ether miners are now known as "stakers".

First, this trade involves something in the future and involves something conditional. This is not possible to do with Bitcoin. But in Ethereum, such functionality is built in and can be run on the Ethereum blockchain.

Second, more importantly, it is interesting to note that without this Ethereum program, this deal otherwise cannot happen between two strangers over the internet. Over the internet, there is nothing preventing the Ethereum holder from reneging on the deal to transfer the Ether after seeing the Bitcoin transfer. However, if such a deal is programmed and then sent into the Ethereum blockchain, it will compute as instructed, with miners fighting to execute each line of the code for reward. The contract would be public and transfer of the Ether would be automatic if the Bitcoin was transferred. This is the key development of Ethereum and forms the notion of a "contract" between two or more parties who otherwise have no trust in each other to contract and no recourse in the case of contract breach.

That Ethereum enabled this trade that otherwise could not happen is a feasible economic basis for Ethereum and smart contracts. Contracting over the internet would otherwise be a gap that Bitcoin alone could not implement. Furthermore, these smart contracts are based on a notion of digital commitment and thus are capable of a software solution. The Economic Layer of Ethereum appears to have significant merit.

A question of importance to society now arises. Assuming the system works in a technical sense, is a smart contract an actual contract in law? Because if a smart contract first conceivably into the legal notion of a contract, then significant progress was made to extend the ability to contract over the internet.

7.3   Smart Contracts as Valid Legal Contracts[2]

Some observers are against interpreting smart contracts as legal contracts (Mik, 2019). But it is important to start from the basics of what constitutes a valid legal contract. The four traditional elements of a valid contract are agreement, consideration, intention, and certainty. These are considered in light of the Bitcoin/Ether trade example earlier.

---

[2] Every legal system would have the concept of contract. Legal discussion here relates to English common law tradition. Despite differences, similar thinking are likely to arise in other legal systems.

Agreement between the parties. This element of a valid contract is often confirmed by seeing one party making an offer and then the other party accepting it. The principle is that there is agreement. There is no over-arching requirement for contracts to be written or signed, but legislation can require such formalities (for example, transfers of land or high value contracts may need to be in writing to be valid).

In the Bitcoin/Ether trade, if the two parties are sending such a program to the Ethereum blockchain to run, along with their respective digital signatures to their Bitcoin and Ether accounts, then agreement must have been present.

Consideration. In relation to contracts, the element of consideration typically refers to one party having to pay something for the goods or services of the other party. There needs to be some exchange. An agreement to get something for free is not recognized as a contract. Any type of valuable exchange will suffice, not just money. A one-sided promise without a promise in return is not, in general, enforceable as a contract.

In a deal to swap Bitcoin for Ether, this is clearly an exchange, so consideration exists.

Intention to create legal relations. A valid contract needs to be formed with the intention to create a binding contract between the parties. That is, contracts cannot be formed by accident. So, social situations where agreements are made between friends do not create valid contracts unless they expressly intended such agreements to be contracts.

In the case of the Bitcoin/Ether trade, by writing the deal into an irreversible Ethereum program, the two parties are serious about the deal and clearly intend to be bound by it. Thus, intention exists.

Certainty of terms. As a practical matter, if an agreement is to be a valid and enforceable contract, it needs to be specific and clear enough on what the terms are. Thus, agreements such as "you give me this burger and I will owe you big" would not be certain enough in its terms to be recognized or enforced as a contract.

In the Bitcoin and Ether trade, terms of the trade are clear and certain. In the example, 1 Bitcoin was to be traded for 10 Ether. Certainty exists.

It then seems that a computer program to trade 1 Bitcoin for 10 Ether does, indeed, satisfy the basic elements of a valid contract. At least in this instance, then, a smart contract seems to have enabled a valid legal trade that otherwise could not have happened over the internet. This would be ponderous progress.

There are also possible smart contracts that would not form legal contracts. For example, a program that only transferred Ether at a future date from one address to another would have no consideration from a counterparty. That would be a smart contract that is not a valid contract in law.

7.4   ANONYMOUS OR TRUST-LESS CONTRACTING

The possible validity of smart contracts as contracts in law is significant progress. It means that the economic basis of Ethereum is strong. It allowed contracting between anonymous strangers online or at least parties who otherwise do not find each other again.

While the definition of a valid contract does not require parties to be identified, in practice, enforcement of any contract in law needs identification of the parties. A court cannot enforce a contract against a person that is anonymous or against a person that cannot be reached. A contract where all parties are unknown simply cannot be enforced in any traditional court or tribunal.

In consequence, while Bitcoin might have allowed anonymous payments online, those payments cannot be part of any enforceable contract to exchange for anything in return. This is a substantial problem if one of the economic arguments for Bitcoin is tied to anonymity. If Bitcoin allowed anonymous payment, without smart contracts, there would be nothing to enforce any reciprocal agreement with the other party.

Thus, before smart contracts, anonymity online could only be one-sided. That is, the party paying Bitcoin can be anonymous, but the party supplying whatever the Bitcoin is exchanged for cannot be. A smart contract plausibly solves this problem by allowing both parties to be anonymous.

Anonymity, in fact, is not the major barrier to online contracting. It is more the lack of enforcement mechanisms if one party reneges on a deal. Contract enforcement even between identified parties in the same country is a slow and expensive ordeal. Enforcement of online contracts across different jurisdictions is far more inconvenient. This is particularly the case that many countries also do not have sufficient legal processes, laws, or courts to enforce contracts in any event.

The internet infrastructure has undoubtedly had major impact on life around the world, and people can communicate across jurisdictions online without problem. Increasingly, even payments around the world, via Bitcoin or otherwise, are getting convenient. But contracting across the world has not advanced nearly so quickly, with one key reason being the lack of an effective enforcement system should contracts go wrong.

All contracts done online must still be set within the laws and enforcement powers of some jurisdiction. Those who are online from jurisdictions without good enforcement powers often find little interest from others who are willing to contract with them online. Smart contracts, in theory, can address this meaningful economic gap.

What smart contracts appear to do is to ensure enforcement of simple online contracts that deal with digital transfers as their subject matter. In this sense, they do fulfill the basic legal definition of a contract. Simple contracts that deal with digital transfers can already accomplish a lot. It can perhaps allow a lot more internet trade in digital content, especially with parties from jurisdictions that otherwise have weak contract enforcement infrastructure.

7.5   LIMITATIONS AS CONTRACTS

Smart contracts do have substantial difficulty replacing all traditional contracts. Numerous shortcomings are evident.

First, there is the issue of whether a traditional contract in language can actually be fully expressed in computer code. Transferring Ether in exchange for Bitcoin is clear in computer code, but most contracts are far less amenable to expression through computer code simply because of the meaning of words. For example, "this rental car shall not be used for commercial purposes" is not something that computer code can accurately express, even though the contract would be clear in words as written. After all, computer code was never designed to express real-life meanings such as "commercial". Computer code is fundamentally procedural.[3]

Second, a smart contract needs to be complete. That is, it should foresee all eventualities and have a procedure to deal with each one. In our example of the Bitcoin/Ether trade, there would need to be code on what happens if there was no Bitcoin sent, what happens if Bitcoin was sent late, what happens if Bitcoin was sent by the deadline but due to no

---

[3] The emergence of AI can create the illusion that computers are expressing meaning. But there does not seem to be a physical possibility for computers to understand meaning.

fault of the sender did not reach the address in time, and so on. In the real world, having a gap in the contract can be cured or imputed by a human judge in a court of law or by subsequent agreement between the parties. Alternatively, the parties can choose to adopt a practical approach to forgive any minor breaches after they occur. However, in the world of smart contracts, the parties are not to find each other again. Thus, the smart contract should have all the contingencies written in, because the computer will run them without discretion. Even for such a small trade, the list of contingencies can be quite extensive to be complete. Contingencies in more complex contracts are likely to be impossible to list out.

Third, not all the terms in a contract are equal. Some terms are deemed more important than others. This is something that the parties can specify themselves in a contract. But if not, even courts will say some terms of a contract to be more central than other terms. The breach of central terms can cancel the entire contract, but the breach of peripheral terms can usually be cured by compensation or entirely forgiven. The determination of which terms in a contract are central and which are peripheral is based in common law jurisdictions by past cases that dealt with similar issues. Such gradations of importance in a contract cannot feasibly be incorporated into a smart contract without very fine-tuned programming. A computer program cannot differentiate between a major and a minor breach unless it is told specifically. To a smart contract, a delay of 1 minute is just as much a delay as 1 week unless it is given clear cut-offs.

Fourth, in the law of society, not all contracts are recognized even after they are validly formed. Agreements to commit crime, for example, cannot be enforced as contracts. Smart contracts cannot recognize this. Some argue that the indifference of smart contracts to criminality may be a feature rather than a bug. But criminality is not the only thing that voids a contract. Misrepresentations, mistakes, coercion, undue influence, and other circumstances can all render an otherwise valid contract void or unenforceable in the real world. However, remedies for such defects, which need to go through a court, are not available in the realm of smart contracts if both parties are not to find each other again.

Sixth, there is a lot of law that can override contracts. For example, consumer protection legislation in England is fairly strong under the Consumer Rights Act 2015, and renders void any terms in a consumer contract that are deemed "unfair". The general common law rule against penalties in contracts can also override a contract. But none of these legal doctrines that take priority over contracts can function in a smart contract since the smart contract would not know about such laws.

Fifth, smart contracts cannot generally be renegotiated, which is otherwise very common in the world and serves very practical uses. To effect amended agreements, another smart contract is needed to reverse or modify the effects of the first smart contract. However, in the pure case, the parties to a smart contract are not to find each other again. Thus, smart contracts are final, and cannot be adjusted over time as circumstances evolve. In the real world, many complex or long-term contracts that explicitly anticipate future changes will therefore not be implementable as smart contracts.

Seventh, at the end of the day, smart contracts can only govern digital transactions. While such transactions are expected to increase over time, much of the world deals in the real physical economy. Contracts for physical goods and services are unlikely to be overtaken by smart contracts because such goods and services cannot fall within the automatic enforcement feature of smart contracts. Nothing on a blockchain can force a plumber to work, force a barber to cut hair, or force a teacher to teach, after all. Perhaps more will happen in the future, but the most a smart contract can fully control at the moment is the trigger of a digital task. Enforcement of any contracts involving physical goods or services must still ultimately be forced by existing courts.

Finally, contract disputes, if they arise, often require some kind of judgment taking into account of all the circumstances. There has not yet been an acceptable algorithm to replace a human judge in a court of law. Thus, in the case of smart contracts, there is little to rely on if something does go wrong, in spite of all preventative efforts and even if the proper solution is glaringly obvious to a human.

Hence, while Ethereum and smart contracts made significant progress in online contracting, they are unlikely able to fully replace traditional contracts.

7.6   The Blockchain Layer of Ethereum and Smart Contracts

The Blockchain Layer for Ethereum and smart contracts is fairly clear. The intent is to facilitate contracting online between parties that may otherwise have no enforcement recourse against each other. This contracting mechanism can also allow contracting between anonymous parties, which are otherwise not possible either. In these circumstances, a decentralized blockchain system makes sense, given the unascertained and possibly anonymous users that the system intends to work for.

Furthermore, assuming the smart contract is on an important subject matter, the ability to do the contract at all would outweigh any speed considerations, and thus slower speed should be an acceptable trade-off versus decentralization. However, many enthusiasts believe that "Decentralized Finance" or DeFi trades—such as the Bitcoin/Ether trade discussed earlier—need to be fast at the same time as being decentralized. Hence, while decentralization is accepted for smart contracts and the use of blockchain is justified, many active projects continue to work on the speed or "scalability" issue in relation to smart contracts (see Chapter 3 on Blockchain Scalability Projects).

On the participation incentives, Ethereum has a reward-based token system for processing smart contracts. These participation incentives are aligned to the overall system.

Thus, the Blockchain Layer of Ethereum seems reasonable and made out.

7.7 THE COMPETITIVE LAYER OF ETHEREUM AND SMART CONTRACTS

The competitive basis of Ethereum is established well. Ether has, in fact, become the second-largest token in the cryptocurrency universe behind Bitcoin. Ethereum has a network effect because users would contract with each other on Ethereum and thus there is an element of natural monopolization to discourage competitors or imitators.

The leadership and funding structure of Ethereum is relatively established compared to other blockchain projects currently in existence. The leadership is strong and influential and the long-term governance of Ethereum is arranged in a crowdfunded foundation structure. Funding has been ample and divided between crowdsourcing and commercial interests. As far as blockchain projects go, Ethereum appears to have given governance and funding due consideration. Ethereum seems to be strong on the Competitive Layer. Few other similar blockchain projects are likely to compete with it successfully.

7.8   ETHEREUM AND THE EBC PYRAMID

Ethereum deals with a valid economic problem in that parties unknown to each other cannot contract effectively over the internet because they have no enforcement mechanism. Solving this problem, even in a limited way, has high potential. Smart contracts on Ethereum are able to solve this in simple circumstances. That is already enough to do a lot and gives Ethereum a clear economic basis.

The blockchain justification of Ethereum is also made out. The Ethereum system is effectively a form of decentralized enforcement for smart contracts. Decentralized processing of smart contracts ensures that no single entity can unilaterally stop the running of any smart contract. The responsibility for implementing any smart contract is decentralized into the system. The incentives of staking users in Ethereum are aligned to maintaining the goals of the whole system.

Finally, on competitors, Ethereum enjoys a natural monopoly effect in terms of the network nature of its system. Furthermore, Ethereum seems to be set up with a long-term view in terms of both leadership structure and funding.

The verdict, by the EBC Pyramid, seems overall favorable for Ethereum.

7.9   APPLICATIONS OF SMART CONTRACTS

The versatility of Ethereum's smart contracts has led to further specific applications built on top of Ethereum. This section discusses a few of these categories, showcasing the range of the opportunities that Ethereum opened up. In general terms, all the projects are in relative infancy. The EBC Pyramid is still a useful method to assess these categories of applications to see how much sense they make.

7.9.1   Online Gambling

The first and most obvious use for smart contracts is online gambling. Such an application corresponds to the important features of smart contracts in terms of transparency and automatic enforcement over a diffuse and unknown user base. Smart contracts, by being open in their code, ensure that the random number generators of the game are fair. Then crucially, smart contracts also ensure that winners are indeed paid.

These are the two fundamental hurdles for online gambling between users who are otherwise unknown to each other. Smart contracts on a blockchain conceivably allow users to gamble with each other directly as well as with a commercial gambling entity.

Such a use, following the EBC Pyramid, will have merit on the Economic Layer and on balance also the Blockchain Layer. The Competitive Layer would depend on the specific project. If it were not for gambling regulation in many parts of the world, online gambling would be the most relevant and immediate use for smart contracts.

7.9.2 Prediction Markets

Some of the earlier ideas to use smart contracts are in prediction markets, due to their similarity to gambling.

The concept of prediction markets has been interesting for some time. The concept is that by having a market to bet on outcomes such as political action, sports, or other events, the price can reflect crowdsourced intelligence on the event's likelihood. For example, if a prediction market is trading at $0.75 on a contract that pays $1 if the Democrats win the next US election, then some say the market is reflecting a 75% chance that the Democrats will win the next US election. In a market with many participants, that 75% is a mass prediction or belief. There is economic value in knowing such mass predictions or beliefs about important events.

Smart contracts were initially thought to be suitable to implement such a prediction market. Several blockchain projects tried to implement prediction markets on smart contracts, the most prominent being known as Gnosis and Augur.

However, such blockchain projects have mostly failed to date because of practicalities, notably on how to determine who actually won. In a prediction market of the next US election, for example, who eventually won will be public and common knowledge in the real world. However, getting that information into the blockchain system so that winners get paid is difficult due to incentives. After all, a blockchain is only computer code and it cannot know the result of the election unless it is somehow told. In a decentralized system, what it is told can be the incorrect outcome. The correct outcome cannot be fed into the blockchain based on voting of market participants themselves. Because for an unexpected event that most market participants did not expect, the majority will have incentive to feed the blockchain the incorrect outcome to protect their own prediction contracts. A decentralized prediction market needs to be able to protect the minority who turned out to be correct against the majority, and simple voting cannot accomplish that.

This is an example of a blockchain application where the economic rationale is plausible and the competitive one might be also, but the blockchain motivation failed because individual incentives were not aligned to the integrity of the system as a whole.

Subsequent attempts to fix prediction markets include a project called Chainlink, which uses a complicated series of smart contracts to pay independent and unbiased participants to feed real-world data into the blockchain. The incentives and practicalities of Chainlink shall determine its success, which is not yet entirely clear. But Chainlink, if it succeeds, can indeed resolve a major roadblock in the application of smart contracts for prediction markets.

7.9.3 Decentralized Autonomous Organizations (DAOs), Voting, and Crowdfunding

The third major application for smart contracts has been Decentralized Autonomous Organizations or "DAOs". Smart contracts are able to count votes. The concept is that smart contracts can serve as the guiding mechanism for large-scale collective decision-making, the results of which could then trigger automatic implementation of the referendum result.

While voting cannot easily aggregate complex preferences (Arrow, 1950), it can implement simple binary choices consistently. The standard arrangement for a DAO is to set up an Ethereum account that users can transfer Ether into in exchange for a proportionate vote. This account then has a smart contract that would send the collective funds to another account depending on the outcome of a vote. If the vote passes, the funds will be transferred to the other account to fund a particular project. If not, the code can allow funds to be transferred back to original funding accounts. It would be unclear how the funded project would then be bound to reimburse the original funders later on or how the funders could enforce any type of rights in the fruits of the funded project. Nonetheless, the concept of a DAO initially got a lot of fanfare.

It is unclear if a DAO works. The earliest large-scale project using this concept was called The DAO, which quickly raised $120 million worth of Ether in 2016 (Waters, 2016). This would be a democratically driven venture capital fund. An entrepreneur would put up a proposal for funding. The DAO members would vote on it through The DAO, and if the vote passes, funds would automatically flow to the entrepreneur's account for use. Before any of the funds could be invested, however, hackers diverted about one third of the funds. The DAO then collapsed.

An example where such a DAO effort did succeed was AssangeDAO, a group that collected funding to buy an NFT (discussed next), the proceeds of which were then in-turn donated to support the legal plight of Julian Assange. However, in this case, there was no reliance on using a DAO for voting, making the use of a DAO simply a crowdfunding mechanism.

The situation of a DAO is effectively the existing system of incorporating a company to pool money from investors, who then vote on important matters to direct the company. The ideological difference is that a DAO may technically not have directors, a CEO, or any other management with discretion. Thus, on relevant matters, the DAO would be driven by computer code or voting rather than by the discretion of a management team. The practicality of an organization driven without human discretion or intervention, and only on computer code and voting can be interesting. Except simple cases such as AssangeDAO, which did not even need voting, it is difficult to imagine how pre-written code and voting can effectively direct all activities of an organization in response to unforeseen circumstances. The main obstacle of a functioning DAO is the organizational structure rather than the technical detail.

At the moment, any DAOs in existence are mostly used as a simple vote counter among possibly anonymous participants. It is not clear what economic problem a DAO system solves, regardless of its complexity, because the problems that would face a DAO clearly outweigh any benefits, if there are any benefits to using a DAO. Thus, the economic merits of any specific DAO need to be clearly defined.

7.9.4   Non-Fungible Tokens (NFTs)

A fourth and prominent application out of Ethereum has been the creation of "Non-Fungible Tokens" or NFTs. These technically do not need the functionality of Ethereum, but most NFTs are nonetheless implemented on Ethereum. The concept is grand in that these are digital tokens that indicate "ownership" of digital assets such as a digital photograph. Such tokens are to be transferrable on the blockchain, and thus can be bought and sold.

In principle, NFTs can solve a fundamental problem of copyright recognition and even licensing over the internet. One can imagine a world where digital photographs or videos or other material have owners, who could be transferred a small amount of cryptocurrency whenever a website uses their photograph or digital asset, or whenever someone loads such a website. Furthermore, such copyright ownership can be bought and sold, thereby creating a market for copyrighted digital works. Such a system is fanciful but not impossible with the development of NFTs and rules of the internet.

The reality at the moment is that an NFT is little more than a line on the Ethereum blockchain containing a link to a file stored somewhere online such as on Dropbox or Google Drive. This is because the files themselves are mostly too large to put into the Ethereum blockchain directly. Sometimes, the link itself is the digital asset, in that it does not link to a file but rather to something else online. An example is a link to the first Tweet by Twitter's founder Jack Dorsey which sold as an NFT for $2.9 million in 2021.[4]

Note that anybody can link to the first Tweet or any other file with an NFT without having to own the NFT. Furthermore, multiple NFTs can be created to point to the same file, and such NFTs can be created by people who never bought or held the first NFT.

The first NFT linking to a particular file does create a permanent date stamp of provenance but does not legally come with any type of ownership or even control over the linked file. There is nothing preventing the linked file from disappearing from Google Drive or Dropbox all together. "Ownership" of that link is transferrable on the blockchain, but there are no rights associated with ownership of the NFT. There is then an immediate question of what an NFT does or why anyone would pay money for one.

NFTs reached a boil in 2021 and early 2022, when NFTs of images created by digital artists fetched up to the record price of $69.3 million for the work called Everydays in a direct sale from the digital artist known as Beeple (Brown, 2021). That sale was an auction from Christie's. Beeple also held the third spot for most expensive NFT sold for a work called HUMAN ONE at almost $29 million, also auctioned by Christie's, but

---

[4] Twitter now being known as X.

the NFT for HUMAN ONE came with "non-commercial" rights to a physical sculpture (Christie's, 2021).

This expensive pricing of NFTs is only seen in the world of contemporary art. The price of contemporary art is often driven on the backstories, the branding of the artist, and oftentimes even a personal relationship with the artist. For example, much of the art of Damien Hirst is made by technicians, yet the work of the same technician is priced considerably less without the Damien Hirst branding (Thompson, 2014, 2018).

Indeed, in contemporary art, there have been sales where only the certificate of authenticity is in any sense the product. An example is the candy art pieces by Felix Gonzalez-Torres, where the art is a pile of candy in the corner of the room. Viewers of this art can freely take the candy and the exhibit is replenished from time to time with new candy. Such art is a concept that anyone can replicate. However, such works have been sold to buyers (Thompson, 2014). The "sale" of such art is by the issue and transfer of a certificate with a description of the exhibition concept, signed by the artist. In theory, that certificate can then be sold on again. Holding the authenticity certificate gives no exclusive right over piling candy in the corner of a room, which anyone can do. But the certificate gives a chain of provenance from the original artist, and an intangible right to tell the story of owning that art.

The major NFT sales so far all carry this aspect of intangible backstory. The NFT sales are not about the NFT itself. It would seem at the moment that NFTs are used for nothing more than as a digital version of the authenticity certificate for digital contemporary art. Such an authenticity certificate itself is worthless by itself. The values in such sales do not reflect value in the technology of NFTs but the value for the underlying contemporary digital art, which can have pricing that defies normal explanation.

The utility value of using NFTs as a blockchain application need to be distinguished from the value of the contemporary art itself. There was not a boom in NFTs in 2021, but rather a boom in digital art that happened to use NFTs as a certificate of authenticity. Even if NFTs get adopted widely for digital contemporary art, the value it adds as a technology over and beyond the underlying art appears modest at most. Meanwhile, NFTs' use as a digital intellectual property royalty system is highly speculative but vastly more valuable as an economic basis should that use ever come to fruition.

REFERENCES

Arrow, K. (1950). A difficulty in the concept of social welfare. *Journal of Political Economy, 58*(4), 328–346.

Brown, A. (2021, March 11). Beeple NFT sells for $69.3 million, becoming most-expensive ever. *Forbes.*

Christie's. (2021). Beeple (b. 1981) human one. https://www.christies.com/en/lot/lot-6345173

Jansen, M., Hdhili, F., Gouiaa, R., & Qasem, Z. (2020). Do smart contract languages need to be turing complete? In *Blockchain and Applications. Advances in Intelligent Systems and Computing* (Vol. 1010, pp. 19–26).

Mik, E. (2019). Smart contracts: A requiem. *Journal of Contract Law, 36.*

Thompson, D. (2014). *The supermodel and the Brillo Box: Back stories and peculiar economics from the world of contemporary art.* Palgrave Macmillan.

Thompson, D. (2018). *The orange balloon dog: Bubbles, turmoil and avarice in the contemporary art market.* Aurum Press.

Waters, R. (2016, May 17). Automated company raises equivalent of $120M in digital currency. *CNBC.*

CHAPTER 8

Blockchain Moving Forward

Abstract This short chapter concludes by discussing some of the issues faced by blockchain projects and the likely path forward for those who seek to analyze potential uses of blockchains.

Keyword Blockchain regulation

8.1 Proliferation

The world of blockchain moves quickly. Terminology, prices, and projects all shifted even during the course of writing of this book. However, the basic notion of a blockchain has not advanced as much. Fundamental advances to speed up decentralized processing have also not come through. What has proliferated most in the recent years has been the number of potential blockchain projects.

At least 20,000 public blockchain projects exist today. Many of them are incentivized through public cryptocurrencies. There have been investment funds and venture capital that invest in blockchain. The total market value of known blockchain cryptocurrencies exceeds $1 trillion and cryptocurrencies are traded on over 600 exchanges.[1] This is, by any measure, strong growth in blockchain applications considering that blockchains amount to little more than public spreadsheet files.

8.2   Regulatory Challenges

The growth of blockchain came with a series of controversies and possible illegalities.

One area involved blockchain project funding. Many blockchain projects crowdfunded their launch by selling their own cryptocurrencies in what are called Initial Coin Offerings (ICOs). Such offerings were often done with casual regard to any law. Many projects then turned out to be scams, whereby the promoters simply took the funding (often in Bitcoin) and ran. Some estimates put up to 80% of ICOs in 2017 to be scams (Dowlat, 2018). This drew the scrutiny of regulators such as the SEC in the USA, which maintains that ICOs are security issuances and thus need to be regulated by the SEC. The SEC in the USA have since launched a series of legal prosecutions against identifiable ICO entities for financial regulatory breaches. A major case is SEC v Ripple,[2] and it has yet to finally conclude in court.

Then there have also been controversies that involved cryptocurrency exchanges. Over the years, numerous companies started exchanges for cryptocurrencies.[3] These exchanges were not subjected to regulation until quite recently. Such exchanges have lost client assets. There have been numerous instances of successful hacking (e.g. BBC, 2018; Chow, 2022; Dougherty & Huang, 2014; Hui & Zhao, 2020; Rizzo, 2014; Zhao, 2019) as well as at least one known incidence where the exchange's CEO died mysteriously taking all the exchange's cryptocurrency passwords with him (Vigna & Shifflett, 2019). Lately, the management of one exchange known as FTX has been charged with fraud for taking cryptocurrency

---

[1] The latest market figures can be see at www.coinmarketcap.com.

[2] An interim judgment is SEC v Ripple Labs Inc 20 Civ. 10832 (AT) (S.D.N.Y. Oct. 3, 2023).

[3] These are not DeFi trades directly between users. These cryptocurrency exchanges ran centralized marketplaces where they processed trades between users.

assets they held on behalf of their clients (Oliver, 2023). Further controversy in the area abounds with allegations such as market manipulation, money laundering, and the use of cryptocurrencies in unrelated scams.

All these developments have drawn the scrutiny of financial regulators around the world, most notably the SEC in the USA. This is in large part because the blockchain ecosystem adopted terminology by analogy to finance and investments, using terms such as "coins", "ICOs" (in homage to IPOs), "exchanges", and so on. If blockchain enthusiasts had adopted less sensitive but equally applicable terminology such as "points", "gifts", "trading clubs", and so on, then blockchains may well have attracted much less attention from powerful financial regulators. After all, blockchain is fundamentally only software. Software—even financial software—is usually not regulated.

The regulatory landscape is moving to protect the blockchain world from scammers and fraudsters. The direction is that exchanges and at least some blockchain projects are to be overseen by financial regulators. This view of blockchains as financial securities is actively being debated and challenged in law. It is unlikely, though, that regulation will in any event shut down blockchains. After all, decentralization was precisely designed to evade legal shutdowns.

8.3 THE IMPORTANCE OF A FRAMEWORK

Our discussion now brings us to reiterate the importance of having a framework to assess blockchain projects for their underlying value and plausibility. For anybody thinking about blockchain projects, there has yet been a systematic framework for their analysis or even discussion. Meanwhile, ever more blockchain projects are emerging and regulation is unlikely to take shape soon to assist in the filtering.

The EBC Pyramid proposed in this book is a series of considerations and questions in the evaluation of a blockchain project (or broader application category). While Ethereum seems to be reasonably founded per this framework, even Bitcoin is unclear on some fundamental questions that the EBC Pyramid raises.

Ultimately and in sum, Blockchain is a valid technology, with potential to do good and address previously unsolvable problems. But blockchain is not applicable everywhere. By going through the layers of the EBC Pyramid and asking at least a couple of key questions at each layer, the plausible and promising blockchain projects might be better separated from the fraudulent, fantastical, misconceived, or otherwise inadequate ones.

REFERENCES

BBC. (2018, January 27). Coincheck: World's biggest ever digital currency 'theft'. *BBC*.

Chow, A. R. (2022, February 10). Inside the chess match that led the Feds to $3.6 billion in stolen Bitcoin. *Time*.

Dougherty, C., & Huang, G. (2014, February 28). Mt. Gox seeks bankruptcy after $480 million Bitcoin loss. *Bloomberg*.

Dowlat, S. (2018, July 11). Cryptoasset market coverage initiation: Network creation. *Satis Group*.

Hui, A., & Zhao, W. (2020, September 26). Over $280M drained in KuCoin crypto exchange hack. *Coindesk*.

Oliver, J. (2023, October 17). FTX deputy says he confronted boss on missing customer billions. *Financial Times*.

Rizzo, P. (2014, March 5). Poloniex loses 12.3% of its Bitcoins in latest Bitcoin exchange hack. *Coindesk*.

Vigna, P., & Shifflett, S. (2019, February 19). 'Our cash went to something': Customers hunt for bankrupt crypto exchange's missing millions. *Wall Street Journal*.

Zhao, W. (2019, March 30). Crypto exchange Bithumb hacked for $13 million in suspected insider job. *CoinDesk*.

Postface—The Interdisciplinary Gap of Blockchain Theory and the EBC Pyramid

Blockchain has seen a lot of coverage from multiple academic disciplines. This is expected because blockchain is a socio-technical invention and it crosses disciplines. This book is an early attempt to discuss and integrate the relevant theories and concepts from different fields that integrate to explain blockchains.

The definition of what is "theory" varies between disciplines. It is sometimes joked that the law school and engineering school do not read each other's publications, because both say the other's work is not theoretical. But from a broad view, the coverage of academic theory in relation to blockchain has fallen into two major streams.

On the one hand, there is literature representing the latest developments of blockchain from different fields.

Academic articles in the field of law, for example, often provide legal commentary on the latest cases in front of the courts. There are major cases going through legal systems now that will fundamentally establish the legal nature of blockchains and the legal relationships between the participants. Questions outstanding in this area include whether cryptocurrencies are securities and whether their holders have any legal relationship such as a partnership.

There are also the important latest developments from engineering. There is engineering literature, both from industry and academia, that aim to solve technical blockchain problems. These are often related to computing speed and security over a decentralized network. Specific protocols, such as the one behind Algorand, have been written specifically to address latest technical blockchain challenges.

Then on the other hand, there is academic literature coverage of blockchain from social science fields such as economics, finance, and information systems that have tried to understand blockchain through the established lines of logic and abstraction from their own field's traditions and theories.

These scholars have used blockchain as a new set of data or case study to shed light on established theories from their respective fields. Information systems researchers, for example, have looked at blockchain from the perspective of technology adoption. Finance academics have examined cryptocurrency prices through their asset pricing theories and models. Economists, broadly, have weighed in from angles such as monetary economics. Political scientists, meanwhile, have looked at blockchain in terms of voting and governance.

Academics tend to specialize, and each field prefers to only publish articles that relate to its own theories. This has led to each academic field to use blockchain to study or reflect on their own theories as opposed to using their theories to shed light on blockchain as its own subject. Because blockchain issues are new and cut across traditional discipline boundaries, understanding blockchain needs a cross-disciplinary framework.

There is yet no conceptual framework to understand blockchain as its own object and its own field, which it now deserves. Indeed, universities have increasingly established cross-disciplinary centers focused on blockchain as its own field of study. Examples include the Centre for Distributed Ledger Technologies at the University of Malta, the Oxford Blockchain Research Centre at the University of Oxford, the Stanford Center for Blockchain Research at Stanford University, the Blockchain Research Laboratory at the University of Edinburgh, and the UWA Blockchain and Cryptocurrency Research Centre at the University of Western Australia. There is an increasing number of others.

This book intended to begin to fill the conceptual gap to provide an overall conceptual framework that establishes blockchain as its own field of study, its interdisciplinary nature, and its theoretical links to different fields. For example, this book discussed the economic basis of Ethereum as creating a new form of anonymous contracting that is not yet legally recognized, and it examined how the technological limits of decentralized processing ultimately prevent its use as a monetary medium of exchange. The reality of blockchains is that it invokes different fields with different levels of importance. Not all concepts from all fields are equally relevant. Yet this perspective cannot be seen from deep within any one field. Understanding this framework of blockchain in its own right will lead to useful progress and applications that can make the best use of blockchains in society and advance its technical capabilities at the same time.

From the overall conceptual discussions, and for practical use, this book presented a summary of the non-technical concepts related to blockchain as the "EBC Pyramid" and further proposed foundations of the non-technical aspects of Bitcoin and Ethereum through this EBC Pyramid.

The EBC Pyramid, and its associated concepts, is a temporary plug in the interdisciplinary gap that surrounds blockchain. Much of blockchain discussion at the moment borrows from other disciplines. As more researchers from both industry and academia begin to realize blockchain as an idea in itself, there will be more research centers, journals, and researchers focused on blockchain as its own field with its own expanding technical and non-technical theory and applications. When blockchain studies mature, there will be a common and accepted body of theory unique to blockchain. The future of blockchain will be academically as well as practically interesting.

INDEX

© The Editor(s) (if applicable) and The Author(s), under exclusive
license to Springer Nature Switzerland AG 2024
S. T. Zhang, *The Potential and Limitations of Bitcoin and Ethereum*,
https://doi.org/10.1007/978-3-031-56783-4